# THE ETHICS OF PEACE AND WAR

# EDINBURGH STUDIES IN WORLD ETHICS

Other titles in the series:

*World Ethics: The New Agenda*
Nigel Dower

*The Ethics of the Global Environment*
Robin Attfield

*Ethics, Economics and International Relations*
Peter G. Brown

*The Ethics of Development*
Des Gasper

# THE ETHICS
## OF
# PEACE AND WAR

## FROM STATE SECURITY
## TO WORLD COMMUNITY

Iain Atack

EDINBURGH UNIVERSITY PRESS

© Iain Atack, 2005

Edinburgh University Press Ltd
22 George Square, Edinburgh

Typeset in Times
by Koinonia, Manchester, and
printed and bound in Great Britain by
MPG Books, Bodmin, Cornwall


A CIP record for this book is available
from the British Library

ISBN 0 7486 2245 4 (hardback)
ISBN 0 7486 1525 3 (paperback)

# CONTENTS

Preface                                                          vii

1. Introduction                                                    1

**Part I International Politics and the Morality of Peace and War**

2. Political Realism and State Violence                           11

3. Internationalism and the Rule of Law                          26

4. Cosmopolitanism and Armed Conflict                            40

**Part II Ethical Approaches to Peace and War**

5. Just War and the State                                        61

6. The Politics of Pacifism                                      76

**Part III Cosmopolitan Strategies**

7. Post-modern War                                               93

8. Human Security, Human Rights and Human Development           111

9. Humanitarian Intervention, Cosmopolitanism and Pacifism     125

10. Peacebuilding and International Conflict Management         141

11. Conclusion                                                  157

Bibliography                                                    160
Index                                                          168

# PREFACE

I read Nigel Dower's book on *World Ethics: The New Agenda* with great interest soon after it was published. What intrigued me most about the book was the application of a general theory about the role of ethics in international affairs to specific issues such as development and peace that were also central to my own concerns. Furthermore, the cosmopolitan approach, with its commitment to a common humanity transcending national or territorial boundaries, also seemed congenial to my own attempts to understand these issues.

Cosmopolitanism seems particularly relevant to the ethics of peace and war because it is perhaps during periods of war and armed conflict that the tensions or contradictions between group or national loyalties and the requirements of a universal moral community become most starkly drawn. One of my hopes at the outset of this project was that cosmopolitanism could provide us with a vital resource for our moral responses to the quandaries and dilemmas thrown up by the nature of armed conflict at the turn of the century. It may help us define much more stringently the conditions under which it is morally permissible to use armed force, for example. Alternatively, it may also challenge us to explore peaceful alternatives to the use of armed force that transcend conventional political structures or forms of social organisation. These themes are examined more closely in the different chapters of this book.

Until recently, international relations theory has focused almost exclusively upon a particular model of the state as the foundation of world order. This has been true of what I have referred to as both 'political realism' and 'internationalism' as theories with implications for the role of ethics in international politics. Cosmopolitanism provides a useful corrective to this focus, partly through suggesting new ways in which individuals and groups can relate to one another in the context of international politics by means of 'world' or 'global' ethics. Thus, it seemed to me after reading Nigel's book that a cosmopolitan or world ethic provided a useful and appropriate framework for beginning my own explorations into alternative approaches to the perennial problems of peace and war.

Translating this general idea into a book was a much more daunting task. Maintaining the balance and the connections between the three general theories about the role of ethics in international affairs and the much more specific problems of war, armed conflict and political violence was a constant challenge. The two chapters on just war theory and pacifism are meant to provide a link between the general theories and the specific issues. While this added to the complexity or difficulty of my task, as I discovered very quickly, it has also allowed me to provide, I hope, a more nuanced and multidimensional depiction of the different levels of debate and argument.

Writing this book has been a tremendous learning experience. It has given me an opportunity to immerse myself, at least intellectually, in some of the most significant ethical and political challenges facing us today. These include the changing nature of armed conflict under the twin processes of state failure and globalisation, as well as establishing the extent of our responsibilities when confronted by massive human rights violations in other parts of the world. On the other hand, sources of hope can be found in expanded concepts of 'human security', as well as recent efforts to implement peaceful methods of 'international conflict management' in the form of peacebuilding and its cognate activities.

I have had the opportunity to share some of these ideas and arguments with friends and colleagues while writing this book. Chapter 9 appeared, in a different form, in *Security Dialogue*, vol. 33, no. 3 (reprinted by permission of Sage Publications Ltd, copyright International Peace Research Institute, Oslo (PRIO) 2002). A version of Chapter 10 was published in *Trócaire Development Review 2003/04* (also reprinted by permission). Comments from anonymous reviewers and editors of both journals helped me refine ideas and arguments in these two chapters.

The Irish School of Ecumenics has been a hospitable and encouraging work environment, and allowed me to circulate in lectures and seminars many of the ideas that eventually appeared in the book. It has always been a privilege to work with such supportive colleagues and such a stimulating group of postgraduate students. In particular, I would like to thank Bill McSweeney for suggesting I 'write a book' and Gillian Wylie for her helpful comments, especially at the book proposal stage.

I would also like to thank Nigel Dower for accepting my request to contribute this book as part of his series on *Studies in World Ethics*, and for his generous provision of critical but helpful comments at the crucial stage. Nicola Carr of Edinburgh University Press has been a model of patience and forbearance, as well as efficiency in terms of the practical side of publishing.

I would like to express my gratitude to my family on two continents for their love and encouragement over the years. My wife Angela contributed the sketch that forms the image for the book cover, and Lochlann and Ruairi provided the necessary distractions and reminded me of the importance of 'play'. Finally, my parents Jim and Margaret instilled in me my love of books and learning and my commitment to cosmopolitan values long before any of us knew what this label might mean.

Iain Atack
Dublin, October 2004

# CHAPTER 1

# INTRODUCTION

## I. GENERAL APPROACH

The purpose of this book is to discuss cosmopolitan responses to the problems of war and armed conflict as apparently intractable and inevitable features of international politics. The hope is that the normative commitment to the equal value of every human being as a member of a universal moral community, which is the defining feature of a cosmopolitan approach to international or world ethics, can facilitate the development of alternative, peaceful and nonviolent responses to political and social conflict.

As such, the structure of the book and its argument is in three parts. In the first section, cosmopolitanism is contrasted with two other theories about the role of ethics in international affairs, political realism and internationalism. While both these theories emphasise the central role of the state and the principle of state sovereignty in international politics, they provide differing and even contradictory positions on the possibilities for ethics in international politics. Political realism argues that norms and values are relevant within states, as moral and political communities, but that this does not extend to the sphere of international politics or international relations. Internationalism, on the other hand, argues that norms can be extended from the domestic to the international realm, primarily by means of the mechanisms or instruments of international law. Both theories about the role of ethics in international relations have specific implications for the possibility of limiting or constraining the use of armed force as a feature of international politics.

The second section of the book looks at two contrasting or contradictory moral positions concerning the use of armed force in international relations: just war theory and pacifism. Just war theory can be interpreted as setting limits to the use of armed force by providing strict criteria for its moral justification, in the form of both *jus ad bellum* and *jus in bello* principles. These two sets of principles determine whether or not it is moral to go to war in the first place (*jus ad bellum*) as well as the morality

1

of belligerent behaviour during war once that decision has been made (*jus in bello*). It can also be viewed as providing sanction or permission for the use of armed force, however, so long as at least some of these conditions are met. Pacifism, on the other hand, involves an unequivocal opposition to the use of armed force for specifically moral reasons. The connections between just war theory and pacifism, and internationalism and cosmo-politanism as more general theories about the role of ethics in inter-national affairs, are also explored.

Finally, these theoretical and ethical positions are applied to particular issues or questions currently confronting states and other political actors in the international arena, such as the nature of contemporary armed conflict or 'post-modern war' and whether or not a 'human security' paradigm provides an appropriate, and cosmopolitan, response to such wars. The book concludes with a discussion of both humanitarian intervention and peacebuilding as potential cosmopolitan strategies for dealing with armed conflict in the current international context.

## II. SOME KEY ISSUES

Thus, the structure and content of the book are such that it requires and provides sufficient background information about wider theories of international relations and the ethics of peace and war to make its specific focus on cosmopolitan responses to war and armed conflict both coherent and credible. Nonetheless, a basic issue or question concerning the role of the state, and the principle of state sovereignty, in either promoting or limiting the use of armed force in the context of international relations emerges from this discussion.

Political realism and internationalism provide different answers to this question. According to political realism, the emphasis on state sover-eignty is responsible for the structure of anarchy that characterises international relations. In the context of this international anarchy, there can be no norms or rules limiting each state's pursuit of its perceived national interest by whatever means necessary, up to and including the use of armed force. For this reason, war and armed conflict are inescapable features of international relations that cannot be constrained or limited by moral or normative considerations.

For internationalists, on the other hand, just as the state is the political mechanism for implementing (and enforcing) the rule of law internally or domestically, it can help to create a similar regime internationally in cooperation with other states. Sovereign states, in other words, are capable of working together to establish and maintain peace and security in the context of an international community characterised by shared norms and agreed laws. In particular, international law in the form of various treaties and conventions can be used to restrain or limit the use of armed force by states as a feature of international politics.

The response of cosmopolitanism to the role of the state can be interpreted in two ways. Cosmopolitanism, which concerns relations between individuals as members of a global moral community, can be viewed as supplementary or complementary to internationalism, which concerns relations between states. Both theories can generate normative or legal restraints on self-interested state behaviour, in the form of a commitment to upholding and maintaining universal human rights or respecting the principle of state sovereignty, for instance, in the context of international politics. This is in the tradition of Kant's version of cosmopolitanism, as outlined in his famous essay on *Perpetual Peace*, with its three levels of *recht* (norms or laws): domestic, international and cosmopolitan.

One difficulty with this integrated interpretation of cosmopolitanism and internationalism, as representing different but complementary levels of laws or norms, is that in practice the governing principle of internationalism, state sovereignty, can come into conflict with universal human rights, for example, as exemplifying the norms and values of cosmopolitanism. This tension between state sovereignty and human rights is at the heart of the UN Charter, which embodies internationalist ideals in so many ways. It is also epitomised more specifically by the ethical dilemma of international humanitarian intervention (discussed in Chapter 9), which involves the deliberate infringement or violation of a state's sovereignty in order to protect the fundamental rights of its citizens.

Cosmopolitanism can also be interpreted as the international ethic associated with revolutionary humanitarian pacifism (discussed in Chapter 6), based on a prohibition against the taking of human life under any circumstances and a rejection of the state as the nexus of organised or institutionalised political violence. This position can be associated with Tolstoy's radical Christian anarchist pacifism, for example.

Thus, the contrast between these two interpretations of cosmopolitanism revolves around differing, and even contradictory, views of the state as a political entity or institution. In one view, the liberal democratic state is a benign instrument for the implementation (and enforcement) of law, and this rule of law can be extended from the domestic to the international and ultimately the cosmopolitan level (Kant). In the other view, the state, defined as the political entity with a monopoly over the use of violence, will inevitably come into conflict with the fundamental rights of individuals as members of a universal (or cosmopolitan) moral community (Tolstoy).

The cosmopolitan response to war and armed conflict depends, ironically, on one's view of the state and whether one adopts deontological or consequentialist approaches to such issues as the deliberate killing of human beings (see Chapter 6). In other words, the contribution of cosmopolitanism as an international ethic to the specific problems of war and armed conflict is contingent upon related issues in political theory and normative ethics. Cosmopolitanism on its own will not provide us with a unique or univocal position on the morality of the use of armed force in international politics.

## III. OUTLINE OF THE REST OF THE BOOK

The book opens with a review of the two dominant theories of international relations: political realism and internationalism (or idealism). It examines their shared emphasis on state sovereignty (also known as the Westphalian model of the state)[1] as the basis of the international system, as well as their contrasting attitudes towards the role of ethics in international relations and the implications this has for the use of armed force.

Chapter 2 discusses the political realist assumption that war is an inevitable feature of international relations because of the combination of state sovereignty, international anarchy and the circumscribed role of morality in international politics. Critics of political realism question this one-dimensional view of state sovereignty resulting in a deterministic interpretation of international relations as a belligerent anarchy, however. This opens up the possibility of other perspectives on the relationship between state sovereignty, international politics and morality, characterised by internationalism.

Internationalism (Chapter 3) stresses the importance of international law and multilateral institutions, such as the UN, as the embodiment of the norms and principles that make a cooperative society or community of states possible. These norms are reflected in international humanitarian law, for example, which governs the conduct of the military during armed conflict and war. Nonetheless, internationalism suggests a tension between state sovereignty and other international norms, such as a commitment to universal human rights.

This tension can become exacerbated or heightened in the context of cosmopolitanism as a third theory about the role of ethics in international affairs, because of its emphasis on the importance of each human being as a member of a global moral community (Chapter 4). Thus, cosmopolitanism has an ambivalent attitude towards both the state as a form of political organisation and the use of armed force or political violence by the state.

Just war theory, discussed in Chapter 5, is perhaps the most coherent attempt to develop a comprehensive set of moral constraints on the use of armed force by the state. Conversely, it also provides a set of criteria for determining the conditions under which the use of armed force by the state is morally justified. Also, the modern discourse of just war tends to be quite state-centred, through its interpretation of such criteria as just cause and legitimate authority, which may limit its usefulness or relevance from a cosmopolitan perspective.

Pacifism involves the renunciation of war for explicitly moral reasons (Chapter 6). This distinguishes it from other forms of antimilitarism, which focus on political, economic or social objections to war. Revolutionary humanitarian pacifism seeks to transcend the nation-state as a form of political organisation because of its intimate links with violence and armed force as its ultimate sanction. This form of pacifism connects to cosmopolitanism, as a theory about the role of ethics in international politics, because they both emphasise and value human beings as part of a shared moral community above exclusive political institutions or allegiances such as the state.

Chapter 7 looks at the way in which armed conflict has continued to change dramatically in the past few decades, particularly since the end of the Cold War. Thus, armed conflicts are now often characterised as 'new wars' or 'post-modern wars', because they so often occur within rather than between states, and because of the prominent role nonstate (or substate) actors play in them. The sovereign state, in other words, may no longer be the key to either understanding or controlling armed conflict as a feature of international politics. This opens up the possibility of either internationalist (in the form of multilateral institutions and 'global governance') or cosmopolitan (in the form of the polycentric dispersal of power through transnational civil society, for example) responses to the problem of war and armed conflict in the new millennium.

The concept of 'human security' (Chapter 8) places the safety and wellbeing of ordinary human beings at the centre of its concern, distinguishing it from the conventional focus on state or national security. It also emphasises the 'soft power' of cooperation and dialogue over 'hard' military power as the best means for obtaining its objectives. Its focus on the needs and rights of individuals in the context of humanity as a whole connects it to a cosmopolitan moral perspective. It may also provide the security paradigm through which multilateral institutions ('global governance') and transnational civil society can respond to new or post-modern wars in the absence of effective state power.

International humanitarian intervention (Chapter 9) may be an instance where a commitment to human security requires the use of armed force. Humanitarian intervention involves external coercive and military interference in the internal affairs of a sovereign state in order to protect the fundamental rights of its citizens. This issue has been at the forefront of recent debates about the role of ethics in international affairs because humanitarian intervention involves an apparent conflict between a commitment to state sovereignty as the basis of international order and our cosmopolitan responsibility to respect and protect the fundamental rights of all human beings. Furthermore, international humanitarian intervention reveals a possible tension between the universal obligations implied by cosmopolitanism and antimilitarist or pacifist objections to the use of armed force.

Humanitarian intervention represents a response by the international community to widespread human rights abuses as the immediate result of either state failure or authoritarian state practices. Peacebuilding, on the other hand, is another type of either international assistance or international intervention that attempts to address the underlying causes of armed conflicts in order to prevent their recurrence (Chapter 10). As such, peacebuilding involves a cosmopolitan commitment to such international norms as human rights and sustainable human development (and to human security more generally). Furthermore, there is an assumption that peacebuilding (and its associated activities such as peacemaking) as components of 'international conflict management' can replace war and armed conflict as responses to social and political conflict. This suggests that peacebuilding could be a crucial component of the cosmopolitan nonviolent strategies of international relations required by pacifism and antimilitarism as alternatives to the use of armed force.

In practice, however, peacebuilding has also been part of the internationalist agenda because of the crucial role the UN and UN agencies have played in its implementation. UN-engineered examples of peacebuilding have involved the transfer of the Westphalian model of the state from 'core' (that is, economically developed) to 'periphery' (that is, economically impoverished) countries. This may exacerbate rather than ameliorate new or post-modern wars where state legitimacy or state control are precisely what is at issue, however.

The focus of the book is to assess what cosmopolitanism, as a theory about the role or place of ethics in international politics, has to say about the specific problems of war and armed conflict and how to resolve or deal with them. This requires a critical comparison between cosmopolitanism and two other equivalent theories, political realism and internationalism, as well as an examination of its relationship with the two main moral responses to the ethical problems of war, just war theory and pacifism. The final suggestion, however unsatisfactory, is that the cosmopolitan response to war and armed conflict is at best ambivalent. The cosmopolitan position becomes more conclusive only in conjunction with other choices or arguments in the realms of political theory and normative ethics.

## NOTES

1. The Treaty of Westphalia of 1648, which ended the Thirty Years War, established the sovereign, territorially defined state as the authoritative political entity or form of political organisation in Western Europe, supplanting the Holy Roman Empire. This model of the state has subsequently taken root or been exported throughout the globe, through processes of decolonisation for example.

# PART I

## INTERNATIONAL POLITICS AND THE MORALITY OF PEACE AND WAR

# CHAPTER 2

# POLITICAL REALISM AND STATE VIOLENCE

Political realism is the doctrine, or type of theory, of international relations that insists that war (or at least the threat of war) is an inevitable feature of international politics. There are three key characteristics of international politics according to political realism: state sovereignty, state security or survival, and state 'self-help', or the zero-sum nature of state interests. In addition to sovereignty, security and self-help, we may add structure (in the form of international anarchy) as a key component of the international system of states, according to political realism. These four characteristics are responsible not only for the inevitability of war, but also for limiting, or even eliminating, the relevance of ethical considerations to international politics.

Thus, Timothy Dunne refers to 'statism', 'survival' and 'self-help' as 'the corners of the realist triangle'.[1] In addition, he refers to international anarchy, or 'the anarchic structure of the international system', as a central characteristic of international politics.[2] This anarchic structure is the product of the central place of the sovereign state, as the supreme political unit, in the international system.

War, and the threat of war, is an inescapable feature of international relations precisely because of state sovereignty and the international anarchy it produces. War becomes a necessary element in the repertoire of instruments of state policy at the level of international politics.

This is linked to a more general argument concerning the limits to normative, as distinct from power, considerations to international politics. Realists can provide a highly sophisticated critique of the role of ethics in international affairs, based on the communitarian emphasis on the significance of moral community, for example, or Morgenthau's concept of 'nationalistic universalism' and Neibuhr's 'double morality'.

Critics of political realism tend to focus on its analysis of international anarchy and zero-sum politics as central features of international relations. At the level of theory, they challenge its positivistic and deterministic assumptions, which severely circumscribe or even eliminate any role for ethics in international affairs. Empirically, they question realism's emphasis on the centrality of the state to both international politics generally and contemporary armed conflict more specifically.

## I. DEFINING FEATURES OF 'POLITICAL REALISM' IN INTERNATIONAL POLITICS

The state is the basic political unit of the international system, for political realism, precisely because of its sovereignty, or the fact that there is no other political entity (such as a world government, for example) that wields power or authority over and above it. It is the presence of this 'multiplicity of independent sovereign states acknowledging no political superior'[3] that produces 'international anarchy' as the basic structure of the international system. Thus, Chris Brown refers to 'the classical doctrine of the two dimensions of sovereignty ... the domestic, in which the sovereign is the source of order, and the international, in which the effect of multiple sovereignties is anarchy'. Order and justice can be sustained internally by the sovereign, while being 'threatened externally by alien violence'.[4]

Furthermore, according to political realism, the economic, political and military interests of each state are both autonomous and competitive, and are pursued ultimately at the expense of every other state. This implies, finally, that national security is the fundamental value or goal of each state, involving most basically its territorial integrity and its survival as a viable political unit or entity. Thus, Martin Wight refers to the state as 'an organization for survival in an international anarchy'.[5]

International relations, almost by definition, involves relations between sovereign states. 'One cannot talk properly about international relations before the advent of the sovereign state.' Furthermore, this is largely a modern, and Western European, phenomenon, at least in its origins. 'This, the state which acknowledges no political superior, largely came about in Western Europe in the time of Machiavelli, at the beginning of the sixteenth century, the threshold of "modern history".'[6] This is the so-called Westphalian model of sovereign, territorially defined nation-states.

Political realism assumes a zero-sum, or competitive and mutually exclusive, interpretation of each state's interests. 'The Realist premise ... is that whatever national interest is, it is likely to be in conflict with other national interests.'[7] It is for this reason 'the Machiavellian', or political realist, 'assumes the desirability of political self-sufficiency', or the 'self-help' approach by states to international politics.[8] Neorealists in particular emphasise that the self-help character of international politics is a function of its structure as anarchy, or its lack of a central authority.[9]

It is also because of this irreconcilability of national interests, according to Wight, that power becomes a central concept for political realists, understood as 'the capacity ... to secure compliance; of states to impose their will, both internally and externally'.[10] Thus, Hans Morgenthau has said: 'International politics can be defined ... as a continuing effort to maintain and to increase the power of one's own nation and to keep in check or reduce the power of other nations.'[11]

Furthermore, this zero-sum interpretation of state interests can be extended to state security as well. Thus, according to Wight, another 'inference is that one power's security is another power's insecurity. There is no general welfare or security ... there is only individual welfare and security, and what one power enjoys another is deprived of.'[12] Just as each state must rely more or less exclusively on itself for the satisfaction of more general national interests, similarly it must be self-reliant in its pursuit of national security. 'For the Machiavellian ... states ... are in a constant state of mutual insecurity, their first concern is, and has to be, self-preservation, and they seek this, so far as they can, by self-sufficiency.'[13]

## II. POLITICAL REALISM AND WAR

There is an intimate link between these defining characteristics of international politics and the inevitability of war and armed conflict, according to political realism. In particular, it is the anarchic structure of international relations, or the multiplicity of independent and competing states in the absence of a single sovereign political entity, that makes war, or at least the threat of war, a permanent feature of the international system. Thus, 'international politics becomes a war of all against all or relationship of pure conflict among sovereign states'.[14] Relations between these sovereign states 'are ultimately regulated by warfare', in the absence of superior authority.[15]

Furthermore, for political realism, state sovereignty is defined and defended, both internally and externally, by the state's capacity to employ force. Thus, according to Dunne:

> For realists, the meaning of the sovereign state is inextricably bound up with the use of force. In terms of its internal dimension, to illustrate this relationship between violence and the state we need to look no further than Max Weber's famous definition of the state as 'the monopoly of the legitimate use of physical force within a given territory'.[16]

In terms of the external dimension of sovereignty, states can be expected to employ force (including military force) both in the pursuit of competitive and mutually exclusive national interests, and also to defend national security, in the form of territorial integrity and the protection of the lives of its citizens.

For political realists, then, war does not represent the breakdown of policy or politics, but rather, in Clausewitz's famous phrase, their continuation by other means. War is simply another instrument available to states, and their rulers, by which they can pursue their interests and objectives in the international arena. As Hedley Bull says: 'From the point of view of the individual state, war has appeared as an instrument of policy, one of the means by which the state's objectives may be attained.'[17]

Thus, Wight outlines 'three particular facets of the Realist doctrine of the conduct of war':

> The first is the belief in preventive war ... The second facet of the Realist doctrine is the acceptance of unlimited war, of the maximum exercise of strength ... The third aspect of Realist doctrine is the destruction of the enemy as the goal of war.[18]

The only limits to the use of war as an instrument of foreign policy are the requirements of the national interest, strategic considerations and material capability.

It is important to note, as Hedley Bull points out, that the state's monopoly over the legitimate use of violence, both internally and externally, represents the containment of violence, for political realists, rather than its proliferation:

> The development of the modern concept of war as organised violence among sovereign states was the outcome of a process of limitation or confinement of violence. We are accustomed, in the modern world, to contrast war between states with peace between states; but the historical alternative to war between states was more ubiquitous violence.[19]

Thus, Hobbes's 'war of all against all' becomes restricted to the international sphere, with states as its only legitimate agents.

Nonetheless, national security is ultimately defined as military security for political realists, giving rise to what is sometimes referred to as the 'security dilemma' of international politics. The best source of national security is military superiority, but because each state pursues its own security in both zero-sum and military terms, this is perceived as a source of insecurity for other states. Wendt points out that for neorealists in particular, 'the inherently competitive dynamics of the security dilemma' result from 'self-help' as a defining feature of the anarchic structure of international relations.[20]

Measures that are intended defensively, such as the Ballistic Missile Defence system of the US for example, are perceived as a military threat by other countries, which then feel it necessary to augment their own military programmes. Thus, this security dilemma is the origin of the arms races and increased tension so characteristic of the international system, as each side seeks either to achieve or protect itself against such military superiority. The nuclear arms race between India and Pakistan is another example of such a security dilemma at a regional level.

E. H. Carr identified this zero-sum search for military security as a primary cause of war and armed conflict. 'The most serious wars are fought in order to make one's own country militarily stronger or, more often, to prevent another country from becoming militarily stronger.'[21] Furthermore, it is difficult to distinguish between wars motivated by this search for security and wars of aggression. 'Wars, begun for motives of security, quickly become wars of aggression and self-seeking.'[22]

## III. POWER AND MORALITY IN INTERNATIONAL POLITICS

Another important implication of international anarchy, or the absence of a sovereign authority within the international system, is that normative considerations, whether legal or moral, are ultimately subservient, at best, to considerations of power and the national interest in the context of international relations. 'Realists ... hold that relations between states are governed solely by power and that morality plays no part in them.'[23] International relations are a realm of necessity, in which the pursuit of power to facilitate and support state survival, rather than ethical or legal norms, is the fundamental criterion governing state behaviour. Hence, according to Hans Morgenthau, 'the flouting of universal standards of morality is not the handiwork of a few wicked men, but the inevitable outgrowth of the conditions under which nations exist and pursue their aims'.[24] The structure of international relations both constrains and is a primary determinant of state behaviour in the international arena.[25]

As Wight suggests, for political realists two criteria govern state behaviour in international politics: necessity and success, where success is determined by state survival and the capacity of a state to protect, and fulfil, its national interests. Furthermore: 'Justification by necessity and justification by success are non-ethical principles.'[26]

The relationship between power and morality for political realists can be more complicated than this simple caricature suggests, however. Communitarian realism, for example, provides a sophisticated account of the connection between the possibility of morality and power politics at the international level.

Communitarianism is the view that norms develop and have meaning only in the context of specific moral and political communities, rather than at the level of some abstract universalism. Combining communitarianism with realism produces the position that morality and law can only occur in the context of states as viable political communities, so that the pursuit of state survival in the international arena becomes self-justifying. States are the ultimate reference points for morality, both domestically and internationally. Power politics creates the conditions under which morality and law can function and exist, in the form of the state. According to Wight, realism 'is implicit chiefly in Hobbes' doctrine that morality and law derive their authority from power, not vice versa ... Power is not subordinate to justice, it is anterior to it'[27] because it creates the political circumstances in the form of the state in which justice can flourish.

It is for this reason that nationalism, understood as the exclusive allegiance by the individual to a particular moral and political community, has become the ideology of the modern nation-state. The nation-state provides the necessary political structure within which moral community can occur. Thus, Morgenthau refers to 'a multiplicity of morally self-sufficient national communities, which have ceased to operate within a common framework of moral precepts'.[28] Similarly, Carr suggests that, for realists: 'Morality can only be relative, not universal.'[29] He connects this view to Hegel, for whom 'states are complete and morally self-sufficient entities ... not united by any mutual obligation'.[30]

Carr goes on to argue that this claim is the most profound challenge that realism presents to 'utopianism', or liberal internationalism. The ethical standards so central to internationalism are not universal norms but 'are historically conditioned, being both products of circumstances and interests and weapons framed for the furtherance of interests'.[31] The rhetoric of international morality, in other words, is merely the projection of state interests.

Not only are these standards and norms the product of circumstances and interests, they are a function of relative power. 'Theories of social morality are always the product of a dominant group which identifies itself with the community as a whole, and which possesses facilities denied to subordinate groups or individuals for imposing its view of life on the community.' This process operates, by extension, at the level of international politics, so that international morality is 'the product of dominant nations or groups of nations'.[32]

Furthermore, any norms that do arise at the level of international relations are merely functions of the anarchic structure of international politics and its competitive nature. 'Normative theorizing can thus not be of any importance [for international politics]; the system operates independently of such theories and itself determines whatever operative normative notions arise.'[33]

According to Morgenthau, attempts to introduce ethics into international politics under such conditions will only magnify, rather than reduce, the causes of war, because of the workings of what he refers to as 'nationalistic universalism':

> Nations ... oppose each other now as the standard-bearers of ethical systems, each of them of national origin and each of them claiming and aspiring to provide a supranational framework of moral standards which all the other nations ought to accept and within which their foreign policies ought to operate ... Compromise, the virtue of the old diplomacy, becomes the treason of the new.[34]

Contrasting (or contradictory) norms and moral practices become a source of conflict and tension between countries or political communities.

A realistic assessment of national interests, which are at least finite and negotiable, becomes clouded or obscured by the limitless demands of a falsely universalistic ideology of irreconcilable nationalisms. As A. J. Coates suggests: ' "Real" war is limited because of its *instrumental* nature and because it relies on political guidance to determine its objectives, objectives that if the realist has his way (and if morality and ideology are kept in check) are always specific and finite.'[35]

Reinhold Niebuhr, the great American theologian of political realism, explained the circumscribed role of ethics for international politics in terms of his famous 'double morality' thesis. According to this thesis, there is a distinction between morality as it applies to individuals and the collective morality of groups. Furthermore, this collective morality applies to state behaviour in international relations. Finally, 'the collective morality of states' is inferior to 'the individual morality of persons'[36] precisely because of the interaction between these two levels of ethics.

Thus, Niebuhr refers to the 'ethical paradox' of patriotism, whereby 'patriotism transmutes individual unselfishness into national egoism'. The 'altruistic impulses' of the citizen are projected on to his or her country as an entity uniquely worthy of loyalty and devotion.[37] Nigel Dower refers, for example, to evidence that 'groups develop strong ties of loyalty within, but hostility towards those outside the group, thus accounting for the immorality of the group in its external relationships'.[38] In other words, individual unselfishness becomes translated into group loyalty or national egoism at the level of the collectivity.

Furthermore: 'The unqualified character of this devotion is the very basis of the nation's power and of the freedom to use the power without moral restraint.'[39] In other words, according to Niebuhr, the moral impulses of the individual in the private sphere become a source of state power, rather than state morality, in the public or international sphere.

Just as the individual citizen feels particular loyalty to his or her country, each state has a primary responsibility 'to secure the interests of the people they serve'. In this view, governments (as 'trustees' of the state), have no right 'to act continuously on any other grounds than national interest ... being agents and not principles'.[40] The primary obligation of the state is 'to promote the welfare, and further the interests' of its citizens, 'and this duty tends to eclipse duty to a wider community'.[41] State survival, 'guaranteed only through rigid adherence to the logic of self-help and power maximisation', is the precondition for its ability to provide for the security and wellbeing of its citizens.[42] Self-interested state behaviour in the context of international politics is a function of each state's obligations towards its own citizens.

The state also has special responsibilities precisely because it is the repository of sovereign, or ultimate, political power both domestically and internationally. This implies, furthermore, 'that there is no authority above the state capable of imposing moral behaviour on it'. One corollary of this lack of a higher or more powerful political authority, according to Carr, 'is that we are bound to concede to the state a right of self-help in remedying its just grievances. Another corollary is the difficulty of securing the observance by all of a common standard.'[43] Thus, the perceived immorality of state behaviour in international politics, in comparison to the standards of individual ethics, is the result of its unique status as a sovereign political entity.

The state's legitimacy as a sovereign entity in international politics is derived from its relationship with its own citizens, represented by the metaphor of the social contract, rather than from any relationship with other states or a higher political (or ethical) authority. This relationship, and its concomitant responsibilities, is the basis of the distinction between killing in war and murder, according to political realists. Thus, according to Hedley Bull, 'what distinguishes killing in war from murder is its vicarious and official character, the symbolic responsibility of the unit whose agent the killer is'.[44] In other words, the soldier who kills an enemy combatant is acting on behalf of the state, which has a specific responsibility to protect the lives of its citizens when they come under threat. It is because the soldier is acting in this official capacity that such killing does not count as murder.

Other ethical considerations (such as a doctrine of just war) are simply not relevant as a source of restraint on military action, neither in terms of justifying or legitimising its use nor limiting the way in which it is employed.[45] Political realists would certainly discount any appeal to the natural law tradition, from which the just war doctrine is derived, as irrelevant to the practice of international politics. Speculations about any metaphysical moral law simply have no impact on state behaviour, particularly in the international realm.[46] Normative considerations are relevant at the level of international relations only to the extent that they can be derived from (or are implied by) state sovereignty, and each state's peculiar responsibility to its own citizens, in the form of the national interest. The state defines the limits of moral community for political realists, rendering the notion of international morality at best illusory and at worst harmful and even dangerous.

Improvements in material capability (military technology) have overcome many of the practical restraints on war, however. As Morgenthau has pointed out: 'The enormously increased destructiveness of twentieth-century warfare, for combatants and civilians alike, is the result of the mechanization of warfare.'[47]

The industrialisation of war has widened the range of strategic targets to include all or most of an enemy country's economic activity, as well as facilitating the ability of the military to attack and destroy such targets. Thus, Morgenthau refers to the 'national interest in the destruction of enemy productivity and his will to resist, as created by the character of modern war, and the opportunity the modern technology of warfare presents of satisfying that interest'.[48] The vastly increased destructive capability of the technology of modern war, including weapons of mass destruction, may require an explicitly moral attempt to limit or even eliminate it as a feature of international politics that the realist approach is unable to provide.

## IV. LIMITS OF POLITICAL REALISM

Those who question the political realist interpretation of international relations tend to focus on its assumptions concerning the central features of international politics, particularly its analysis of the state and of international anarchy. They question the realist view of the sovereign state as a discrete and uniform political unit, for example, as well as the assumption that anarchy implies a state of nature or war of all against all at the international level.

Some critics point out, for instance, that states vary enormously both throughout history as well as currently, and that any interpretation of state behaviour in the international arena must acknowledge these differences. Each state is the product of specific historical, social and geographical factors, and these distinctive features must be included in any account of its position and its role in international affairs. Thus, the situation of Vanuatu cannot be conflated with that of the United States, for example, or Ireland with Russia.

Similarly, as Wight points out, political realism assumes that each state is sovereign, uniform and equal within the international system. It 'is entirely concerned with horizontal relations of state against state; not with the class-structure of states and the class-structure of international society itself'.[49] Quite apart from ignoring the internal dynamics of each country, such as class structure or dichotomies of wealth and power, and how this might affect its role in international politics, political realism also ignores the hierarchy of states within the international system (with the US at its pinnacle) and how this must influence international relations.

These three characteristics of the state (sovereignty, uniformity and equality) within the international system also indicate that states inevitably operate within some sort of normative framework, even for realists. As Mervyn Frost suggests:

> [I]t is not possible to conceive of something as a state independently of its making and recognizing claims based on some code of conduct. Recognizing such rules and being recognized in terms of them is what is involved in being a state.

He concludes that states must operate within some sort of normative framework, and cannot be entirely amoral, simply because such rules or such a framework are partially constitutive of what it is to be a state.[50] State sovereignty, for example, is not merely a political structure or institution. It is also a normative concept implying the acceptance of certain rules or standards of state behaviour.

The state, at its core, is a normative entity, implying 'the existence of a group of people who are in some way bound together, in large part, by a set of normative commitments and obligations'.[51] Even power, the central feature of politics and the state, 'always exists within a practice which is partially constituted by certain normative ideas'.[52]

Historical sociologists also question both the uniform and ahistorical interpretation of the state presented by political realists, as well as their deterministic interpretation of the relationship between sovereign state and international structure. According to historical sociologists, the modern state is a function of war instead of the other way round. In other words, the modern state evolved into its current form to meet the institutional and political requirements of war-making.

> War plays this central role because it is through preparing for war that states gain their powers as they have to build up an infrastructure of taxation, supply, and administration. The national state thus acquires more and more power over its population by its involvement in war.[53]

Thus, the nation-state as we know it today is the product of specific historical forces and has evolved to support particular activities associated with war. War as a feature of international relations has produced the modern nation-state, inverting the relationship between the two ascribed by political realism.

Others criticise the determinism that links the political realist emphasis on the sovereign state to its view of international politics as a lawless and belligerent anarchy. Alexander Wendt, for example, argues 'that self-help and power politics do not follow either logically or causally from anarchy'.[54] He suggests that social structures, including the structure of the international system, are constructed, rather than politically or socially determined. In other words, states (and other international actors) are in a position, to some extent, to create an international sphere in their own image, or at least the image they wish to project upon it. International anarchy as a state of nature is not an inescapable and foregone conclusion. In Wendt's well-known phrase: 'Anarchy is what states make of it.'[55]

Wendt's social constructivist response to the political realist interpretation of international politics focuses on how state identities and interests are 'formed in the process of interaction' between states, 'rather than being formed prior to interaction'.[56] Constructivists, in other words, 'think that structure is the product of social relationships', and that such relationships are influenced by 'ideational' factors,[57] such as 'shared understandings, expectations, or knowledge', and not just by material interests and capabilities.[58]

Material interest, for example, does not determine the nature or structure of international relations as an anarchic and zero-sum war of all against all. Instead, international relations, or the interactions between states, help shape or construct each state's view of its interests. These in turn help shape or construct the structures and institutions of international politics. State identity and interests are not given, or predetermined, so neither are the institutions or structures of international politics. 'Self-help', for instance, or the zero-sum approach to state interests, is only 'one such institution, and is therefore not the only way of combining definitions of identities and interests in conditions of anarchy'.[59]

Wendt argues decisively that self-help is a contingent rather than a logical feature of anarchy as the structure of international relations.[60] 'Self-help is an institution, one of various structures of identity and interest that may exist under anarchy.' Furthermore, an institution 'is a relatively stable set or "structure" of identities and interests ... Institutions are fundamentally cognitive entities that do not exist apart from actors' ideas about how the world works.'[61] In other words, 'ideational factors' in the form of identities and interests influence the way in which states behave towards one another even in the context of international anarchy. Wendt concludes that 'we cannot derive a self-help structure of identity and interest from the principle of anarchy alone'.[62]

Similarly, Wendt contrasts the security dilemma, as 'a social structure composed of inter-subjective understandings' based on mistrust between states, with a security community, 'composed of shared knowledge in which states trust one another to resolve disputes without war'.[63] In other words, the security dilemma is not an inevitable feature of the international system, even one characterised by anarchy.

Such an interpretation of international politics has important implications for the role of normative theory, and of ethics, in international relations. As Frost points out: 'Normative theory always presupposes that actors [including states] in the practice of international relations do have alternatives and real choices, and can change their conduct.' Furthermore, 'normative theory in international relations presupposes that the international order itself can be deliberately changed in specified ways'.[64] It is only if states have genuine choice in the conduct of their relations with other states that ethics becomes relevant to international politics.

Others question the political realist identification of security with state survival or national security, particularly when this is defined in military or militarised terms. The suggestion is that the focus of security concerns should be individuals or at least human beings, via the protection of human life for example, rather than on the security of political entities, such as the state. Furthermore, the argument goes, the excessive emphasis on the military security of the state is in fact a primary source of threat to human life and wellbeing. This view of 'human security' will be discussed in Chapter 8.

Perhaps the most timely critique of political realism as a theory of international relations, in the context of contemporary discussions of globalisation in particular, concerns its emphasis on the centrality of the state, understood as a sovereign and universal political entity. This Westphalian understanding of the nation-state, as a discrete political and geographical (territorial) entity is now an anachronism, if it ever was entirely accurate.

> This model is now mute when it comes to expressing the transformations that have been taking place as a result of the processes of globalization. Other models are now tested: empire, cosmopolis or 'governance'.[65]

'Empire' refers to the unprecedented global dominance of a single superpower, the US, following the demise of the Soviet Union and the end of the Cold War. The cosmopolitan viewpoint emphasises the role and place of the individual as a member of a universal moral (and political) community, while 'governance' is based on the pre-eminence of international institutions such as international law or multilateral organisations.

Cosmopolitanism and multilateral internationalism in particular each focus on a different level of analysis than does political realism, the one substate (cosmopolitanism) and the other suprastate ('governance' or internationalism). Their views on war and peace will be contrasted with those of political realism in subsequent chapters of this book.

The failures, and limitations, of the political realist view of the state are shown most graphically, perhaps, in the context of the changing nature of war and armed conflict (discussed in more detail in Chapter 7). John Baylis writes, for example: 'The fracture of statehood is giving rise to new kinds of conflict within states rather than between states which the state system cannot deal with.'[66]

The most obvious example of the changing nature of armed conflict, however, is perhaps 11 September 2001 and its aftermath.

> The 'war against terrorism' is a kind of conflict that cannot be explained through Westphalian categories … It is not a struggle among peers – equally legitimate Leviathans – but a conflict in which the actors are intrinsically heterogeneous. The conflict that opened up after 9/11 makes it impossible to continue to think of war in traditional terms.[67]

Transboundary war is no longer international war, in the sense of occurring between sovereign states. The state no longer exercises a monopoly over the use of force at this level, if it ever did, in accordance with the political realist theory of international relations. The state, in other words, does not occupy a unique position in contemporary discussions about war and peace.

## NOTES

1. Dunne, 'Realism', p. 110.
2. Ibid. p. 113.
3. Wight, *International Theory*, p. 7.
4. Brown, *International Relations Theory*, p. 130.
5. Wight, *International Theory*, p. 104.
6. Ibid. p. 1.
7. Ibid. p. 112.
8. Ibid. p. 144.
9. Wendt, 'Anarchy is what states make of it', p. 392. Wendt contrasts 'classical realism', with its emphasis on 'human nature' as the source of 'egoism and power politics', with structural realism or neorealism, with its emphasis on the anarchic structure of international politics as the source of these features of international politics (p. 395).
10. Wight, *International Theory*, p. 107.
11. Morgenthau, *Politics Among Nations*, p. 237.
12. Wight, *International Theory*, p. 114.
13. Ibid. p. 145.
14. Bull, 'Martin Wight and the theory of international relations', p. xi.
15. Wight, *International Theory*, p. 7.

16. Dunne, 'Realism', p. 114.
17. Bull, *The Anarchical Society*, p. 186.
18. Wight, *International Theory*, pp. 220–1.
19. Bull, *The Anarchical Society*, p. 185.
20. Wendt, 'Anarchy is what states make of it', p. 392.
21. Carr, *The Twenty Years' Crisis 1919–1939*, p. 111.
22. Ibid. p. 112.
23. Ibid. p. 153.
24. Morgenthau, *Politics Among Nations*, p. 259.
25. Cf. Frost, *Ethics in International Relations*, p. 55.
26. Wight, *International Theory*, p. 250.
27. Ibid. p. 103.
28. Morgenthau, *Politics Among Nations*, p. 257.
29. Carr, *The Twenty Years' Crisis 1919–1939*, p. 21.
30. Ibid. p. 153.
31. Ibid. p. 68.
32. Ibid. p. 79.
33. Frost, *Ethics in International Relations*, p. 54.
34. Morgenthau, *Politics Among Nations*, pp. 259–60.
35. Coates, *The Ethics of War*, p. 25.
36. Holmes, *On War and Morality*, p. 55.
37. Niebuhr, *Moral Man and Immoral Society*, p. 91.
38. Dower, *World Ethics*, pp. 29–30.
39. Niebuhr, *Moral Man and Immoral Society*, p. 91.
40. Wight, *International Theory*, p. 242.
41. Carr, *The Twenty Years' Crisis 1919–1939*, p. 159.
42. Bellamy, 'Humanitarian Intervention and the Three Traditions', p. 10.
43. Carr, *The Twenty Years' Crisis 1919–1939*, pp. 160–1.
44. Bull, *The Anarchical Society*, p. 184.
45. See, for example, Coates, *The Ethics of War*, pp. 22–3, 24.
46. Wight, *International Theory*, p. 235.
47. Morgenthau, *Politics Among Nations*, p. 374.
48. Ibid. p. 246.
49. Wight, *International Theory*, p. 143.
50. Frost, *Ethics in International Relations*, p. 47.
51. Ibid. p. 58.
52. Ibid. p. 63. He writes, furthermore, that: 'Power is … based on cooperation according to norms' (p. 66).
53. Smith, 'New Approaches to International Theory', p. 179.
54. Wendt, 'Anarchy is what states make of it', p. 394.
55. Ibid. p. 395.
56. Smith, 'New Approaches to International Theory', p. 185.
57. Ibid. p. 186.
58. Baylis, 'International Security in the Post-Cold War Era', p. 204.
59. Smith, 'New Approaches to International Theory', p. 185.
60. Wendt, 'Anarchy is what states make of it', p. 396.
61. Ibid. p. 399.
62. Ibid. pp. 423–4.
63. Baylis, 'International Security', p. 204.
64. Frost, *Ethics in International Relations*, p. 52.

65. Spini, 'Reflections on Death, Fear and Security', p. 507.
66. Baylis, 'International Security', p. 208.
67. Spini, 'Reflections on Death, Fear and Security', pp. 507–8.

# CHAPTER 3

# INTERNATIONALISM AND THE RULE OF LAW

Internationalism involves the view that the rule of law provides the basis for world society, unlike realism, which claims 'there is no "international society", only a war of all against all'.[1] It stresses that 'not only conflict but also cooperation' features in international politics, which can be described therefore not as 'international anarchy but as international intercourse'.[2]

Internationalism argues that the rule of law, as the basis for international cooperation and security, is a central feature of international politics. This stands in stark contrast to the realist depiction of international relations as a realm of anarchy, dominated by the competition for national power.

Furthermore, it suggests that the use of armed force can be contained, although not eliminated, through agreed norms embodied in international law. Typically, this has taken the form of translating just war criteria into the secular instruments of international humanitarian law. A cosmopolitan critique of internationalism revolves around the tension between its continued commitment to state sovereignty and the requirements of the norms embodied in international law (such as human rights, for example).

## I. INTERNATIONALISM AND INTERNATIONAL LAW

According to Timothy Dunne, liberal international idealism 'rests on a domestic analogy'.[3] In other words, just as the rule of law and the institutionalisation of politics is vital to establishing peace and security domestically, or within states, so it is also necessary to achieve peace and security internationally, or between states.

> Idealists seek to apply liberal thinking in domestic politics to international relations, in other words, institutionalise the rule of law. This reasoning is known as the domestic analogy.[4]

Michael Walzer, for example, uses the domestic analogy as the basis for his discussion of the 'legalist paradigm', which in turn provides the scaffolding for his analysis of 'law and order in international society'.[5] The analogy is sometimes but not always pursued to the extent of arguing in favour of a world government as the required institutional context for international law.

A related view is the so-called 'democratic peace theorem', or the view that democracies are much less likely to go to war with each other. According to this view, democracies are more likely to settle international disputes by means of agreed rules in the context of multilateral institutions, rather than through the use of armed force, partly because they share domestic norms concerning the rule of law and the institutionalisation of politics by peaceful means. In other words, the 'domestic analogy' is more than just an analogy, because the internal structure of states has implications for their behaviour internationally.

The principle of 'the rule of law' is central to both domestic and international law. 'The essence of this principle is that everyone is equal before the law.'[6] In a domestic context, this principle is applicable to all citizens, while in an international context it is applicable to all states, where it gives rise to the further principle of the sovereign equality of states. According to this fundamental principle, all states are legally equal in the context of international law, no matter their size in terms of territory or population or material capability.

Nonetheless, as Shirley Scott points out, there are two 'important distinctions between the domestic legal system of liberal democratic societies and the system of international law'. The first is that 'there is no international legislature to pass legislation and "make law"'.[7] The other is that 'there is no international police force to enforce compliance'.[8]

Scott identifies two sources of international law in the absence of an international legislature: treaties (or conventions) and custom. Custom, as a source of international law, refers to state behaviour, or 'what states do'. The relevance of custom, or state behaviour, to the creation of international law is determined by the principle of *opinio juris*, according to which the 'practice of a state can be used as evidence of custom only if ... the state has been choosing to act in that way for reasons of law'.[9] In other words, arbitrary or perniciously self-interested state behaviour cannot be used to establish customary international law.

Scott refers to the elimination of the Taliban regime in Afghanistan by the US following the events of 11 September 2001 as an example of the way in which state behaviour has 'confirmed an evolution of customary international law to include a right to use force in self-defense against a terrorist attack'.[10] Following the campaign, 'it could be said that customary international law has evolved such that the right of self-defense now includes military responses against states that actively support or willingly harbor terrorist groups', even where the state itself may not be directly involved in the attack.[11]

The lack of an international legislature contributes to a further distinction between the status of states under international law and of citizens under domestic law, based on the principle of consent. Domestic legislation is binding on citizens whether they agree directly to it or not, whereas states are not bound to treaties to which they are not a party. This is because of the sovereignty of the state within the international system, so that states cannot be coerced into conforming to rules to which they have not agreed. Or, as Scott phrases it in legal terms, 'a state is, by definition, *constitutionally independent*, which means that a state must *consent* to be bound by a treaty before it becomes bound'. The extent of state constraint under international law is summed up by the principle of *pacta sunt servanda*, according to which 'states are bound to carry out in good faith the obligations they have assumed by treaty'.[12]

Scott does question the 'absolutist acceptance of the principle of consent', as applied to state obligations under international law, on the basis of *jus cogens*. '*Jus cogens*, or "peremptory norms" of international law, are those rules – widely considered to include the prohibition against the use of force in article 2(4) of the UN Charter as well as those against aggression, genocide, and slavery – that have come to be accepted so widely that they are considered to be compulsory for all states.'[13] These rules, which seem to be prohibitions rather than obligations, have evolved to provide a vital normative framework for the international system of states, and are binding on all states on that basis.

Scott provides several criteria for defining statehood. These include 'a permanent population, a defined territory, and a government', as well as its 'capacity to enter into relations with other states' derived from its 'sovereign independence'. The most important *de facto* criterion 'in an anarchic state-based system', however, 'is that a state is a political entity that other states accept as being a state'.[14]

*De jure*, in terms of international law, 'confirmation of the territorially defined state as the basic unit at the international level is usually dated from the Treaty of Westphalia of 1648'. In other words, the 'territorially defined state is generally regarded as having originated in Europe' with a treaty that ended 'the political dominance of the Roman Catholic Church'.[15]

The distinction between 'naturalist' and 'positivist' explanations of the authority of law applies to international law as much as it does to domestic law. Naturalists argue that this authority resides in 'principles of natural law that exist independently of people'. International law is ultimately subordinate to this natural law (as is domestic law).[16] Positivism, on the other hand, 'is the belief that law is made by people', who do not deduce it or derive it from any higher source. In the international realm, then, international law is nothing more nor less than what states make it to be, according to positivism.[17]

Realists tend to align themselves with positivist explanations of law, and of international law in particular, according to which law is merely a function of power politics and perceived self-interest. Internationalists, on the other hand, tend towards naturalist explanations of law, according to which it can provide a genuinely independent standard for assessing the behaviour of both states and individuals. Scott identifies Hugo Grotius, 'often regarded as the founder of modern international law', with the naturalist tradition, for example.[18]

Martin Wight argues that internationalists (whom he refers to as Grotians or Rationalists) 'derive international law equally from the law of nature and from existing practice and agreement among nations', that is, from a combination of natural law and custom.[19] This 'naturalist tradition', according to Wight, holds that 'the sovereignty of states in the international community and the absence of any common superior does not involve pure anarchy', contrary to the claims of realists, 'because prior to all political organization there still exists law, based on reason and the nature of man as a social being'.[20] Thus, according to E. H. Carr, it was under the auspices of natural law 'that modern international law was created by Grotius and his successors to meet the needs of the new nation-states'.[21]

In addition, 'the primary evidence of what that law is is custom, the existing practice of all nations'.[22] Thus, 'in the Rationalist tradition, international law is conceived as the existing practices and treaties of states, constantly refined by references to certain fundamental standards and norms of which they are the imperfect expression'.[23]

The internationalist holds that such custom, in the form of agreed norms (sometimes embodied in international law), as distinct from power (as the realist would argue), 'is the dominant mode of intercourse between nations'.[24] Wight goes on to argue, however, that for the internationalist 'an even distribution of power', or a balance of power, is nonetheless a necessary condition of a viable system of international law, because of the absence of a central political authority above sovereign states to enforce this law.[25] Such an even distribution, or balance, of power renders power ineffectual as an instrument of foreign policy, and allows for the rule or implementation of international law in its place. It is also the case, however, as Wight points out, that it is in the interest of lesser powers to insist on both the priority of international law and its normative basis: 'small powers are normally the chief spokesmen of general principles, of moral law and natural law, because they have no other defence'.[26]

## II. INTERNATIONALISM, PEACE AND WAR

The internationalist emphasises the importance of the rule of law partly because they do not succumb to the realist zero-sum interpretation of security. According to Wight, the internationalist (or Rationalist) separates security from national power, so that all countries can move simultaneously towards security, as they can towards prosperity, within a system of international law.[27]

Security can be achieved cooperatively and not necessarily competitively, and this makes international law possible. Furthermore, establishing a viable rule of law internationally is one crucial component of security of potential benefit to all countries. Thus, it has been suggested that policies of either collective or common security, reinforced by multilateralism and international law, are necessary to escape the 'security dilemma' implicit in the realist interpretation of security, especially in the age of nuclear weapons and other weapons of mass destruction.

Nonetheless, internationalism views the use of armed force as 'a necessary evil, to be minimized as much as possible',[28] because it is the ultimate method for enforcing international law. Furthermore, Hedley Bull suggests: 'International society is now reluctant to view war as law enforcement except in cases where it is resorted to for reasons of self-defence.'[29] The use of armed force, in this sense, can be distinguished from war between states in pursuit of conflicting perceptions of the national interest.

According to Martin Wight, 'the doctrine of the just war' is central to the liberal internationalist (or 'Rationalist') 'theory of the purpose and conduct of war'.[30] Any 'theory which ... maintains that war may be waged only with economy of means, and that there are strict limits to what is permissible in war ... is in the Rationalist tradition', as distinct from the realist advocacy of the necessity and inevitability of total war.[31] Just war theory, in other words, provides the norms and principles that form the basis of international law as it is applied to war and the use of armed force.

Grotius 'inaugurated the modern development of international law' through his 'attempt to restate and revive the criteria of just war' in a secular format.[32] Just war theory provides both *jus ad bellum* and *jus in bello* criteria concerning the use of armed force in international relations. *Jus ad bellum* principles provide criteria for determining when it is just to go to war, while *jus in bello* principles provide criteria for assessing the behaviour of belligerents in their conduct of war. These are discussed in more detail in Chapter 5.

International law seeks increasingly to codify just war principles (both *jus ad bellum* and *jus in bello*) in legal terms. Mervyn Frost suggests, for example, that peace as a norm 'is built into international law in the *ius ad bello* which narrowly restricts the circumstances under which states may resort to war'. Furthermore: 'This norm is also a bedrock norm underpinning the United Nations charter.'[33] Another writer claims that 'the laws of war ... are a remarkable pact crafted by military leaders and humanitarians to limit the methods and means of war and thereby human suffering',[34] in accordance with *jus in bello* requirements.

*Jus in bello* components, 'imposing limitations on the conduct of hostilities', were the first to be incorporated in international law, specifically international humanitarian law.[35] International humanitarian law, in other words, is that aspect of international law incorporating *jus in bello* requirements, or restrictions on the conduct of war. The significance of international humanitarian law from a cosmopolitan perspective is that it supplies universally applicable 'rules for the treatment of the individual – civilian or military, wounded or active – in international armed conflicts'.[36]

On the other hand, war was accepted as a feature of international politics following the institutionalisation of the sovereignty of the state in the Treaty of Westphalia. The 'right to resort to arms was considered an important attribute of state sovereignty', obviating the need for *jus ad bellum* considerations, since the decision to go to war was purely a matter for each state. 'It was acceptable, where necessary, to utilize force', providing it was employed in accordance with contemporary *jus in bello* requirements.[37]

Nonetheless, the last century saw some attempts to incorporate *jus ad bellum* criteria, concerning decisions to initiate war or the use of armed force, into international law. The main *jus ad bellum* requirements under contemporary international law are provided by the UN Charter, which permits the use of armed force under only two circumstances: self-defence (article 42) and the protection of international peace and security as determined by the Security Council (article 51).

The key components of international law concerning the use of armed force over the last century or so include the two Hague Conventions of 1899 and 1907, the 1928 Briand-Kellogg Pact outlawing wars of aggression, the UN Charter (especially article 2(4)), and the Geneva Conventions (1949).[38] It has been suggested, however, that 'the legal texts concerning use of force have ... undergone little, if any, change since the adoption of the UN Charter in 1945'.[39]

The principle of discrimination, or noncombatant immunity, is an important example of a *jus in bello* principle that has become a central feature of international humanitarian law. Thus, according to Hans Morgenthau:

it is considered to be [both] a moral and legal duty not to attack, wound, or kill noncombatant civilians purposely ... The Hague Conventions with respect to the Laws and Customs of War on Land of 1899 and 1907, and the Geneva Convention of 1949, gave express and virtually universal sanction to that principle.[40]

In the context of the modern state system, the combatant–noncombatant distinction, in legal as well as moral terms, rests on the view that war occurs between sovereign states, and combatants are legitimate targets only insofar as they are agents of the state.

Article 48 of the first protocol to the Geneva Conventions (1977) 'codifies the *principle of distinction*', or noncombatant immunity:

> In order to ensure respect for and protection of the civilian population and civilian objects, the Parties to the conflict shall at all times distinguish between the civilian population and combatants and between civilian objects and military objectives and accordingly shall direct their operations only against military objectives.[41]

This is supplemented by other articles relevant to noncombatant immunity. Article 51(5), for example, expresses the proportionality qualification of the principle of double effect through prohibiting 'an attack which may be expected to cause incidental loss of civilian life, injury to civilians, damage to civilian objects ... which would be excessive in relation to the ... military advantages anticipated'.[42] (The principle of double effect is discussed in more detail in Chapter 5.)

Dinah PoKempner, general counsel at Human Rights Watch, suggests however that this 'core tenet of international humanitarian law – the distinction between combatants and non-combatants', is under threat from current US military strategy in the context of the so-called 'war on terror'. The US insists that 'civilian morale is a legitimate target in war', for example, because of its current emphasis on 'the political objectives of war' instead of battlefield operations. It has targeted broadcasting stations, for instance, as purveyors of 'propaganda to the population', even though international humanitarian law 'strictly prohibits attacks against civilians and civilian infrastructure'.[43]

The second major field of international law concerning war and armed conflict, as distinct from humanitarian law, are arms control treaties between states. These can be both multilateral, as in the case of the Nuclear Non-Proliferation Treaty (NPT), and bilateral, as in the Anti-Ballistic Missile (ABM) Treaty between the US and the Soviet Union (and its successor states) that was in force for three decades until it was abrogated by the administration of George W. Bush in 2001.

Arms control treaties, although they concern the limitation of weaponry, are not derived from just war principles in the same way that international humanitarian law is. As Scott points out, however, there can be some overlap concerning these two types of international law, 'even though arms control treaties do not directly address what happens when there is armed conflict'. The Ottawa Convention on landmines, for example, could count as both a contribution to international humanitarian law and as an arms control treaty.[44]

## III. SOME CONTRADICTIONS OF INTERNATIONALISM

Both realism and cosmopolitanism focus on the tension between the norms (embodied in international law) characterising the international system according to internationalists (such as principles of human rights, for instance), and its continued commitment to state sovereignty as the basis of world order. This tension is at the core of the Charter of the United Nations, for example, an organisation representing perhaps the supreme political achievement (however constrained or curtailed) of internationalism in practice. Realists resolve this tension in favour of state sovereignty, or at least the primacy of the national interest. Cosmopolitans, on the other hand, try to resolve it in favour of universal norms that transcend the limits of state boundaries as exclusive moral and political communities.

From a realist perspective, it is mistaken to think of international relations producing a genuine moral, legal or political community. Carr, for example, suggests 'it would be dangerous to suppose that this hypothetical world community possesses the unity and coherence of communities of more limited size up to and including the state'. He argues that this is mainly for two reasons:

> (i) the principle of equality between members of the community is not applied, and indeed is not easily applicable, in the world community, and (ii) the principle that the good of the whole takes precedence over the good of the part, which is a postulate of any fully integrated community, is not generally accepted.[45]

It is precisely the huge variety of and disparity between states that prohibits the achievement of genuine equality between them in the context of a multilateral system. Similarly, so long as sovereign states remain the primary political entity within international politics, they will ultimately pursue their own partial goods where these conflict with the putative good of the whole system.

This latter point is illustrated by the distinction between treaties or international agreements and laws as products of legislation. As Carr points out, treaties or international agreements are voluntary contracts entered into by states with each other (in accordance with the principle of consent). They are 'not laws created by states in the capacity of international legislators' that are 'unconditionally applicable to all members of the community whether they assent to it or not'.[46] As voluntary contracts, such treaties are a reflection of each state's perceived self-interest. They do not reflect state acceptance that such self-interest can be superseded by involuntary obedience to the law, because it embodies the good of the whole of the international community.

Furthermore, according to Carr, the 'positivist or realist view of law' defines it simply 'as a command', without any normative or ethical basis as such.[47] Thus, international treaties or agreements can be considered law only to the extent that they contain some element of coercion or enforcement, and not because they somehow embody the normative aspirations or ideals of a mythical international community.

Carr is also quite critical of the suggestion that international law can somehow contribute to creating an international community. He argues that politics precedes law in the sense that 'law is a function of a given political order'.[48] Systems of law are one part of more comprehensive political institutions, and cannot be created in a political vacuum. Those political institutions currently embody the sovereignty of the nation-state, and so must law. International law, in other words, can only reflect the perceived national interests of those states creating it by means of political processes such as treaty negotiations and custom (in the form of state behaviour in the international arena). 'It follows that the strengthening of international law, and the extension of the number and character of international disputes recognised as suitable for judicial settlement, is a political, not a legal, problem.'[49] It will only occur through changes to the political institutions and power relations making up the international system.

Carr concludes that the 'condition of international legislation is the world super-state', whose authority supersedes that of individual nation-states so that its 'decrees will be recognised as binding on states without their specific assent'.[50] In other words, international law as a substitute for war and armed conflict as a way of dealing with inter-state disputes requires the suppression of state sovereignty.

Cosmopolitanism, on the other hand, might question the circumstances under which internationalism permits the use of armed force. It preserves the use of armed force as an inescapable feature of the international system of sovereign states, even if this is constrained or circumscribed by either just war theory or international law. As Hedley Bull points out, there is a fundamental ambiguity between 'the perception of war as a threat to international society which must be contained' and the use of armed force to enforce international law, preserve a balance of power and so on, on behalf of sovereign states.[51]

This is related to the cosmopolitan criticism that internationalism continues to privilege the state over the individual in the context of world society, because sovereign states remain the primary components of the international system. Scott confirms, for example, that:

> States are the most important actor in the system of international law. As we have already seen, state practice gives rise to custom, and interstate negotiations produce treaties.[52]

Even those alternative interpretations of security, such as collective security and common security, which focus on multilateralism and the rule of law as a way out of the security dilemma, retain the state as the primary referent of security. The result is that the interests of the state and the preservation of the state system can be pursued at the expense of individual human rights, for example.

Scott does emphasise the centrality of the United Nations, as an inter-governmental or multilateral organisation (or, more accurately, 'complex institutional network'[53]), to international law. 'The United Nations is ultimately inseparable from the contemporary system of international law.' In practical terms, 'hundreds of treaties have been concluded by UN organs or by diplomatic conferences convened by the UN'. Furthermore, in legal terms, the UN Charter is supreme in international law, superseding other treaties where there might be a conflict between them. Both the Charter and the UN itself are also extremely comprehensive in terms of the subjects or topics they address.[54] Scott suggests that 'the UN Charter plays a role akin to the constitution of the international community' because it 'contains rules, principles and concepts fundamental to the contemporary system of international law', such as 'the peaceful settlement of disputes'.[55]

The UN also represents a limitation of the sovereign independence of its member states. Under article 25 of the UN Charter, for example, 'member states agree to carry out the decisions of the Security Council; this means that the Security Council has legal power over states'.[56]

Nonetheless, the UN is an inter-governmental organisation, however idiosyncratic because of its near universality and comprehensiveness. Its membership is made up of states, which retain their ultimate sovereignty within the international system. The UN can do no more than its member states permit it to do, so that decision-making power remains ultimately with states as sovereign political entities.

As Mervyn Frost suggests, within the state system the primary duty of 'the government of a sovereign state' is 'to protect the interests of its own citizens'. This takes priority over any concern over 'the well-being of people elsewhere in the world' in the name of universal human rights.[57]

On the other hand, according to Scott, 'while international human rights law and sovereignty may often seem to be juxtaposed, in practice the implementation of effective human rights policies is not possible in a weak state'.[58] While this may be true in terms of the domestic implementation of human rights, however, there remains a significant tension if not contradiction between state pursuit of perceived self-interest and universal human rights at the level of international politics.

Frost is critical of those, such as Michael Walzer, who attempt to derive 'the rights of states ... from individual human rights' via some sort of social contract. The irreducible or irresolvable tension between state sovereignty and human rights is revealed by the debates surrounding humanitarian intervention, for example, as Walzer himself is forced to concede in *Just and Unjust Wars*.[59] These debates are examined more closely in Chapter 9.

For Frost, there seems instead 'to be a basic tension between those norms concerned with the preservation of the system of states and sovereignty on the one hand, and those norms related to individual human rights on the other'.[60] Frost reverts to a constitutive (or communitarian) rather than contractarian understanding of the relationship between rights and state sovereignty, according to which 'a person is constituted as a rights holder of a certain sort within the context of a specific social relationship' such as the state, rather than viewing the state as a device for protecting 'certain pre-existing rights'.[61]

Frost, in other words, defends state-centric discourse in the context of ethical perspectives on international relations precisely because state legitimacy and state sovereignty cannot be derived from individual human rights. Thus, he suggests 'any discussion about what ought to be done in world politics ... must be conducted in the language of the modern state system. No other language is available'.[62]

The cosmopolitan, on the other hand, might be suspicious of both contractarian and communitarian attempts to justify the primacy of the state within the international system in terms of its role in protecting human rights on empirical as well as philosophical grounds. The cosmopolitan accepts Frost's elaboration of the contradictions between state sovereignty and universal human rights because of the state's inevitable pursuit of the national interest, but argues instead that we need to find some way of institutionalising the primacy of human rights independent of the state or exclusive moral and political communities.

In addition to this cosmopolitan normative critique of the state-centrism of internationalism, it can also be criticised because it does not reflect the circumscribed role of the state in the contemporary international context (sometimes referred to as globalisation). This is true even in terms of the regulation or containment of war and the use of armed force.

> Strictly interstate *jus ad bellum* (and the charter paradigm is one hundred percent state-centric) does not fit well with the changed international system where non-state, sub-state and super-state actors play an important role.[63]

The 'charter paradigm' here refers to the rules concerning the use of armed force set out in the UN Charter.

Thus, it has been suggested that the greatest challenge confronting humanitarian law today 'is the regulation of *noninternational*, or internal, armed conflicts', or conflicts within rather than between states, where states or governments are at most one protagonist among many. Some protection was extended to noncombatants in the context of internal armed conflicts by means of the 1949 Geneva Conventions and their 1977 Protocols.[64] Similarly, the increasing economic and political power of transnational corporations as a central feature of processes of globalisation is a challenge to the state-based nature of international law.[65] This includes the use of private militia to protect their interests, as has occurred in oil and natural gas producing areas in Nigeria and South America, for example.

Furthermore, the actions of Al Qaeda demonstrate the significance of nonstate actors in armed conflict that is neither internal nor international, but is nonetheless transboundary. Thus, Bull argues that: 'International society will not be able to afford to allow these new forms of war to lie permanently beyond the compass of its rules.'[66] The continuing US military pursuit of Al Qaeda in Afghanistan and elsewhere also raises issues in terms of Charter definitions of 'self-defence' under Article 51 for example.[67]

Thus, internationalism shares with realism an acceptance of the state as the supreme or ultimate political entity in the context of the international system. Cosmopolitanism challenges this state-centrism on both philosophical and empirical grounds. Philosophically, such state-centrism reconciles the tension between state sovereignty and individual human rights in favour of the state. Empirically, it does not confront the fact that states are sometimes the most serious threats to the fundamental human rights or civil rights of the citizens they are meant to represent and protect, precisely because it reserves for itself a monopoly over the use of armed force. Furthermore, it does not recognise the diminished power or role of the state in the context of contemporary forms or instances of the use of armed force or political violence, a subject to which we will return in Chapter 7.

## NOTES

1. Wight, *International Theory*, p. 139. The most the realist, or 'Machiavellian', can hope for is 'a state-system, a diplomatic system, which is an arena of power politics'.
2. Bull, 'Martin Wight and the theory of international relations', p. xii.
3. Dunne, 'Liberalism', p. 152.
4. Ibid. p. 161.
5. Walzer, *Just and Unjust Wars*, pp. 58ff.
6. Scott, *International Law in World Politics*, p. 13.
7. Ibid. p. 3.
8. Ibid. p. 7.
9. Ibid. p. 6.
10. Ibid. p. 7.
11. Ibid. p. 9.
12. Ibid. p. 6.
13. Ibid. p. 301.
14. Ibid. p. 22.
15. Ibid. p. 23.
16. Ibid. p. 89.
17. Ibid. p. 90.
18. Ibid. p. 89.
19. Wight, *International Theory*, p. 233.
20. Ibid. p. 234.
21. Carr, *The Twenty Years' Crisis 1919–1939*, p. 173.
22. Wight, *International Theory*, p. 234.
23. Ibid. p. 237.
24. Ibid. p. 39.
25. Ibid. pp. 166, 167.
26. Ibid. p. 131.
27. Ibid. p. 129.
28. Ibid. p. 206.
29. Bull, *The Anarchical Society*, p. 198.
30. Wight, *International Theory*, p. 217.
31. Ibid. p. 259.
32. Ibid. p. 217.
33. Frost, *Ethics in International Relations*, p. 109.
34. PoKempner, 'Bending the Rules', p. 14.
35. Scott, *International Law in World Politics*, p. 103.
36. Ibid. p. 245.
37. Ibid. p. 103.
38. See Müllerson, '*Jus Ad Bellum*', pp. 151–2.
39. Ibid. p. 150.
40. Morgenthau, *Politics Among Nations*, pp. 241–2.
41. Cited in Scott, *International Law in World Politics*, p. 251.
42. Ibid. p. 251.
43. PoKempner, 'Bending the Rules', p. 14.
44. Scott, *International Law in World Politics*, p. 245.
45. Carr, *The Twenty Years' Crisis 1919–1939*, p. 162.
46. Ibid. pp. 171, 172.
47. Ibid. p. 176.

48. Ibid. p. 178.
49. Ibid. p. 199.
50. Ibid. p. 211.
51. Bull, *The Anarchical Society*, p. 188.
52. Scott, *International Law in World Politics*, p. 21.
53. Ibid. p. 35.
54. Ibid. p. 36.
55. Ibid. p. 65.
56. Ibid. p. 37.
57. Frost, *Ethics in International Relations*, p. 108.
58. Scott, *International Law in World Politics*, p. 299.
59. Frost, *Ethics in International Relations*, pp. 132–3. See also p. 137.
60. Ibid. p. 137.
61. Ibid. p. 138.
62. Ibid. p. 90. See also p. 79.
63. Müllerson, '*Jus Ad Bellum*', p. 155.
64. Scott, *International Law in World Politics*, pp. 250–1.
65. Ibid. p. 297.
66. Bull, *The Anarchical Society*, p. 199.
67. See Müllerson, '*Jus Ad Bellum*', pp. 176ff.

# CHAPTER 4

# COSMOPOLITANISM AND ARMED CONFLICT

Cosmopolitanism refers to the view that as individuals we are all part of a universal moral community. It is commonly contrasted with communitarianism, which holds that all ethical systems are irrevocably embedded in specific moral communities or traditions.

Cosmopolitanism has both ethical and political dimensions. Consequentialism, deontology and rights-based approaches are each examples of cosmopolitan ethical theories within the Western philosophical tradition. Politically, cosmopolitanism implies a critique of the central role of state sovereignty in political theory and international relations.

The tension between cosmopolitan and communitarian approaches to ethics, or the moral claims of universal humanity and the demands of national or group loyalty, is especially evident in times of war and armed conflict. Cosmopolitanism can support specific principles of moral restraint during war and armed conflict associated with just war theory, such as proportionality and discrimination. It may also provide a more general moral framework or justification for the renunciation of war associated with pacifism.

## I. DEFINING CHARACTERISTICS OF COSMOPOLITANISM

Cosmopolitanism refers to those normative ethical theories that advocate a universal (or 'world') ethics for all human beings as members of a single moral community.[1] According to David Held, cosmopolitanism rests on the principle (or assumption) that: 'Humankind belongs to a single moral realm in which each person is equally worthy of respect and consideration.'[2] In other words, as human beings we are members of a universal moral community, and all moral claims are to be treated equally or assessed impartially regardless of cultural, political or geographical boundaries.

As such, cosmopolitan ethical theories can be said to share three important characteristics: egalitarianism (or impartiality), individualism and universality (or inclusiveness). According to John Charvet, for example:

> A cosmopolitan ethical theory, as I understand it, holds that there is an ideal moral order that applies universally and in which individual human beings are immediately members. As such they have rights and duties in relation to all other human beings ... Contemporary conceptions of a cosmopolitan ethics defended in mainstream English-speaking philosophy are standardly [sic] said to be egalitarian and individualist. By this is meant that the source of moral worth in those conceptions is the individual person and individuals are held to be equally valuable beings.[3]

The principle of egalitarianism implies impartiality in the sense that our obligations are determined by an equal consideration of the claims of every person affected by our moral choices.[4] According to Charles R. Beitz, cosmopolitanism 'applies to the whole world the maxim that choices about what policies we should prefer, or what institutions we should establish, should be based on an impartial consideration of the claims of each person who would be affected'.[5]

Held also suggests that the fundamental cosmopolitan principle of 'moral egalitarianism' is further connected to 'the principle of reciprocal recognition', according to which each person is required to respect the equal moral worth of every other person.[6] Similarly, Buchanan and Keohane refer to this as 'a core commitment of the cosmopolitan ethical perspective: *mutual respect* for all persons'.[7]

Cosmopolitanism is conventionally contrasted with communitarian normative theories. Cosmopolitanism and communitarianism are usually taken to be contradictory ethical positions, in the sense that either one or the other must be true, and normative theories therefore fall into either one category or the other. Communitarianism limits one's primary obligations to the members of a particular community, defined 'in terms of established traditions, felt relations and shared values'.[8] Furthermore, according to Dower, 'what is important ... to the communitarian approach is ... that these facts about the social constitution of ethical norms provide us with the key to their justification. Ethical norms are justified precisely by being embedded in custom, convention and tradition.'[9] In other words, ethical norms are not merely created by specific moral communities, they can only be justified by reference to them.

This focus on the particularity of community as both source of and justification for ethical values and principles contradicts the aspirations towards both universality and impartiality characteristic of cosmopolitan theories. Thus, Toni Erskine suggests that for communitarian normative theories 'moral reasoning is necessarily *situated*, *embedded* and *embodied*.[10] The cosmopolitan principle of impartiality, in particular, is challenged by the notion that all individuals, as moral beings, must be placed in a specific social and political context. The communitarian insistence on context contradicts the cosmopolitan position that impartiality 'requires abstraction from particular ties and loyalties' and 'an impersonal standpoint from which equal consideration can be given to all'.[11]

This challenge to cosmopolitanism merely adds to the political 'suspicion that claims of impartiality in moral reasoning behave as no more than a façade for the cultural and political imperialism of those with power'.[12] In other words, if an impartial and universal moral stance is an impossible ideal, then one is justified in asking whose special interests are masquerading as cosmopolitan moral claims. This resembles the realist critique of the use of moral language in international politics associated with E. H. Carr, for example.

Carr also refers somewhat sceptically to the connection between cosmopolitanism, natural law and reason, derived from the Stoics and reappearing in modern times through the ideals (and idealism) of the European Enlightenment, epitomised by Kant. The assumption, of course, is that human beings can determine 'universally valid moral laws' through the exercise of reason, and that somehow these shared laws or principles will help us overcome conflict based on narrow or parochial state or group interests.[13] There is also an assumption that human beings, whether individually or in groups, will act on these principles once they have been rationally established or determined.[14]

One of the problems with a communitarian approach from a cosmopolitan perspective, however, is that it is exclusive, partial and conservative. It is difficult to establish, for example, how a particular set of practices (such as slavery, for instance) sanctified from within or even constituted by a specific moral tradition or community can be challenged, except possibly on the grounds of internal coherence, since external criticisms are simply not relevant.[15] Similarly: 'Feminist critics of communitarian political thought make the point that the morally constitutive community is often a realm of oppression and exclusion' because of prescribed and highly unequal gender roles and so on.[16] Finally, the tension between abstract, universal and impartial principles and values originating in and given meaning by a particular moral context, exemplified by the contradictory positions of cosmopolitanism and communitarianism, is especially evident during situations of war and armed conflict, with the demands of national loyalty on the one hand competing with the claims of universal humanity on the other.

## II. TYPES OF COSMOPOLITANISM

Dower identifies some of the most influential theories throughout the history of Western philosophical ethics as cosmopolitan. These include 'utilitarianism, Kantianism, and natural law theories and the later modification and extension of these into human rights theories'. Utilitarianism is probably the best-known version of a consequentialist approach to ethics, which emphasises our unique obligation to maximise (or at least optimise) the amount of good in the world as a result of our actions. Deontological normative theories, on the other hand, of which Kantianism is a prime example, hold that the maximisation of the good as the result of our actions is not the only general principle relevant to their rightness or wrongness. [17]

Although these theories are profoundly different and even contradictory in many respects, they share a cosmopolitan commitment to the universal applicability of their principles regardless of community or national loyalties or boundaries. 'The natural tendency of these theories is to advocate some kind of world ethic for individuals, as belonging to one moral community.'[18]

The intellectual origins of the term (as its etymology suggests) go back to the Stoics of classical Greek and Roman philosophy. According to Martha Nussbaum, the Stoics held that: 'We should view ourselves as fundamentally and deeply linked to humankind as a whole, and take thought in our deliberations, both personal and political, for the good of the whole species.' In addition to their universalism, the Stoics were also committed to the ethical equality of 'each and every human being, just in virtue of being rational and moral'.[19] Furthermore, the equal and inalienable dignity of every human being exists independently of and prior to any particular legal or political order.[20] At a minimum, members of this universal moral community have an obligation of nonmaleficence, or 'fundamental, perfect or non-optional duties not to harm one another'.[21]

Kant revived these themes in his moral philosophy. Thus, for Kant all human beings have equal moral standing because of their status as rational, autonomous moral agents, or 'ends in themselves'. Furthermore, these individual moral agents are in direct relation to one another as equal members of a universal moral community. Nussbaum claims, for example, that 'Kant appropriates ... the idea of a kingdom of free rational beings, equal in humanity, each of them to be treated as an end no matter where in the world he or she dwells' from the Stoics.[22]

The distinctiveness of Kant is that he refers to the autonomy of the will, or the self-legislating individual, as the ultimate source of moral laws,[23] as distinct from external authority in the form of natural law or the Stoic *logos*. In other words, self-legislating individuals, through their common rationality and the autonomous exercise of their wills, can arrive at universally valid and universally applicable moral principles.

Held refers to the significance of what he calls 'the metaprinciple of autonomy' as a 'justificatory rationale' for cosmopolitan egalitarianism.[24] In other words, this emphasis on each person as a moral agent generates the cosmopolitan 'preoccupation with each person as a subject of equal moral concern'.[25]

Kant also used these themes in his discussion of the problem of peace and war in international politics. In the analysis of 'cosmopolitan right' in his essay on 'Perpetual Peace', for example, Kant famously claims: 'Because a ... community widely prevails among the Earth's peoples, a transgression of rights in *one* place in the world is felt *everywhere*.'[26] Furthermore, for Kant the moral autonomy of individuals through which they arrive at universally applicable ethical principles can only be secured and reflected in a political order governed by the rule of law. Domestically, this requires 'a constitutional state' where 'conflict might be so regulated that each citizen may be free to reason for himself'.[27] Internationally, this requires or implies the abolition of war, understood not merely as open armed conflict but also as the enduring threat of the use of military force by one state against another. The abolition of war and its replacement by the rule of law is essential to achieving security and justice for all human beings.[28]

The critical theory of Jürgen Habermas, and his discourse ethics in particular, is sometimes presented as a contemporary restatement of the Enlightenment ideals associated with Kant, because of its emphasis on 'rationality and the sovereignty of the human subject'.[29] Habermas also insists, for example, on the universalisability of valid moral principles. 'Where discourse ethics differs from Kant's formulation is that, for Kant, universal applicability was the result of private reasoning on the part of the philosopher', whereas 'discourse ethics ascertains the validity of norms in a process of discourse and argumentation between genuine concrete, situated agents'. Proponents of discourse ethics as a cosmopolitan moral theory suggest that it is able to overcome the dichotomy between its abstract universalism and the embedded and exclusive moral traditions of communitarianism precisely because it does not prescribe 'substantive moral content'. It provides, instead, 'merely the correct procedures for determining which norms can be said to apply to all' on the basis of a conversation or dialogue between equals.[30]

Thus, a cosmopolitanism based on discourse ethics 'does not require the creation of a completely homogeneous society that is dismissive of group and particularistic identities'. It argues, instead, 'that individuals embedded in particular contexts are nonetheless capable of thinking in universalist terms' and can determine through debate and discussion with others the content of a cosmopolitan ethic.[31]

Utilitarianism, unlike Kant, focuses on consequences rather than intentions as the moral basis of action. Nonetheless, according to Chris Brown, the utilitarian calculus, or 'greatest-happiness principle of utilitarianism', is 'both universal and cosmopolitan'.[32] Our sole obligation is to ensure our actions maximise (or at least optimise) happiness for all human beings equally everywhere. Utilitarianism conforms to the three defining characteristics of cosmopolitanism (universality, individualism and equality) because: 'It says that all human beings are to count as having the same moral weight, and that in coming to a decision we have to take into account the effects on anyone, however far away they are, psychologically or geographically.'[33]

The contemporary focus on human rights in the context of both domestic and international politics is another important example of a cosmopolitan ethical approach. As Dower suggests: 'A human right exists in virtue of a universal moral theory which postulates the whole world as one moral sphere or community.'[34] David Held links cosmopolitan 'egalitarian individualism' to human rights: 'the requirements that each person be treated with equal concern and respect, irrespective of the state in which they were born or brought up, is the central plank of the human rights world-view'.[35] Thus, the term 'human' as applied to rights is not a mere 'pleonasm', or a redundant use of words, as Kant claims the word 'perpetual' as applied to peace is.[36] Instead, the term 'human' indicates the true universality of these rights, because 'these are entitlements ascribed to human beings everywhere'.[37]

Such universal human rights must be clearly distinguished from 'a legal or conventional right which exists in virtue of the laws and conventions of a given society. People have conventional rights as members of a legal community, not as human beings.' Human rights may be encapsulated in aspects of international law such as the Universal Declaration of Human Rights, but are nonetheless both ethically and logically distinct from such legal formulations, however important they might be as embodiments of a cosmopolitan or world ethic.[38]

## III. POLITICAL IMPLICATIONS OF MORAL COSMOPOLITANISM

Cosmopolitanism as an ethical theory, with its emphasis on universality especially, can present a profound moral challenge to conventional political structures and theories. This is because, according to Chris

Brown: 'What is crucial to a cosmopolitan attitude is the refusal to regard existing political structures as the source of ultimate value.'[39] Or as Molly Cochran phrases it: 'Cosmopolitans, like liberals, value individual autonomy, and this value is prior to any value placed on the associations that compartmentalize humanity.'[40] Kant, with his vision of 'the individual as a moral agent existing prior to society', epitomises this view.[41] The state has at best a purely instrumental value, derived from its capacity to facilitate the exercise of individual moral choice and to serve human ends. Loyalty to humanity as a whole should always supersede loyalty to a state or a particular political community, where these come into conflict.

The primacy of state sovereignty in conventional international relations theory, for example, would be threatened by an unambiguous or unequivocal commitment to ethical cosmopolitanism. As Dower points out:

> National boundaries do not, with this approach, have any ultimate moral significance ... There is, therefore, either explicitly or implicitly, a challenge to the idea of absolute loyalty to one's own state.[42]

Similarly, Erskine suggests: 'state borders and community boundaries must be morally irrelevant from the perspective of impartialist cosmopolitanism'.[43] And according to Nussbaum, this conforms to the Stoic perspective that 'we should give our first moral allegiance to *no* mere form of government, no temporal power. We should give it, instead, to the moral community made up by the humanity of all human beings.'[44] Thus, we can connect the ethical and the political dimensions of cosmopolitanism without insisting that ethical cosmopolitanism as such implies one particular type of political structure, such as a world government.[45]

The notion of the state, and state sovereignty, as the central components of international relations is challenged by the cosmopolitan suggestion that individuals have moral obligations, and rights, that transcend national boundaries. This does not require the dissolution of an international system based on states as discrete political entities through the establishment of some sort of 'world republic' or super-state. It does require, however, that the behaviour of states be circumscribed by international law, or the 'law of nations'. Kant suggested this through including international 'right' as part of his threefold analysis of the rule of law (or *recht*) in 'Perpetual Peace'. In particular, Kant is associated with the so-called 'democratic peace', or the view that an expanding federation of law-abiding and democratic (or 'republican') states is the best route to achieving world peace.

Unlike Hobbes, Kant argues that the same logic that drives human beings to establish the rule of law, or domestic right, within states, namely the need for security, will also drive states to establish the rule of law internationally. The internal stability of a state depends upon the integrity and security of its external relations. Kant 'is convinced ... that the will to minimize violence in favor of general codes of conduct' that exists between individuals in the context of the state 'will also arise between states'. He sees this 'as a rational necessity arising from each state's ultimate desire for internal security'.[46]

Daniele Archibugi emphasises the interdependence of domestic and international order, contrary to the realist position, for example, which emphasises their independence from one another. In particular, Archibugi argues that 'domestic democracy cannot fully mature in a world marked by conflict' because of the threat posed by international violence to the state. A primary task of proponents of both domestic and cosmopolitan democracy must be to control this violence.[47]

A vital component of Kant's project for 'perpetual peace', furthermore, is his commitment to cosmopolitan law, or a 'law of peoples,' governing those obligations we have towards any human being, and not merely our fellow citizens. Kant restricted this to a duty of hospitality towards foreigners, although in our contemporary era of mass migration (including political refugees as well as economic migrants) fulfilling even this limited requirement could have far-reaching implications.

It has also been suggested, expanding perhaps on Kant's original vision, that 'human rights must be the domain of cosmopolitan law, which institutionalises basic rights of individuals and the rule of law at the supranational level'.[48] The human rights of each individual have a moral, and legal, status that transcends their position as citizens of a particular country or state. As Habermas says: 'The point of cosmopolitan law ... is that it goes over the heads of the collective subjects of international law to give legal status to the individual subjects and justifies their unmediated membership in the association of free and equal world citizens.'[49] The 'collective subjects of international law' are, of course, sovereign states. David Held claims that the Universal Declaration of Human Rights 'marked a turning point in the development of cosmopolitan legal thinking' because it recognises individuals, and not just states, 'as subjects of international law'.[50]

One implication of this is that governments have a fundamental obligation to respect, protect and promote the basic rights of all human beings, not just those of their own citizens, in accordance with the cosmopolitan ideal. As Dower suggests, cosmopolitanism implies that 'governments ought in their foreign as well as domestic policies, to further the realisation of human rights'.[51]

Thus, Kant viewed the three levels of the rule of law, republican (internal or domestic), international and cosmopolitan, as providing the essential foundations of world peace. Martin Wight's image of three concentric circles can be used to illustrate the relationship between Kant's three types of 'right' or law.

> A picture began to emerge of the three concentric circles; the inner circle was the state, with its municipal law, or 'jus civile'; the second circle was international society, subject to a volitional, positive law of nations; and the third, outer circle, surrounding the other two, was mankind, subject to natural law.[52]

Wight's image suggests the priority of cosmopolitan law over the other two types of law, which are somehow contained within it. Furthermore, his description suggests the ultimate supremacy of natural over positive law. Both conditions seem vital to the success of the cosmopolitan project.

Brohman and Lutz-Bachman argue that this project involves a shift away from a conventional interpretation of state sovereignty as the basis of global order in favour of 'a democratic sovereignty of citizens that is differentiated and polycentric'.[53] Furthermore, Habermas argues that far from undermining or diminishing the authority of the democratic state, such 'polycentrism' can complement and perhaps reinforce it:

> Cosmopolitan law is thus a consequence of the idea of the constitutional state. In it, symmetry is finally established between the juridification of social and political relations both inside and outside the state's boundaries.[54]

In this sense, pluralising sovereignty, or the rule of law, is a positive-sum rather than a zero-sum game, in terms of supporting democracy within and peace between states, as well as the universal human rights of all human beings.

David Held agrees that cosmopolitan political institutions do not require the end of the state (although they may require a reinterpretation of sovereignty):

> A cosmopolitan polity does not call for a diminution *per se* of state power and capacity across the globe. Rather, it seeks to entrench and develop political institutions at regional and global levels as a necessary complement to those at the level of the state.[55]

The functional or instrumental value of the state is to be emphasised, along with that of other levels of political community or organisation, as distinct from its priority as the primary unit of political affairs, whether domestic or international.

Habermas suggests that 'the institutions, declarations, and policies of the United Nations' as an inter-governmental organisation have given a 'tangible form' to 'the idea of perpetual peace'.[56] Most important of these, perhaps, is Article 2(4) of the UN Charter, according to which member state renunciation of war as an instrument of foreign policy is a central provision of international law. The Universal Declaration of Human Rights can also be viewed as a cornerstone of cosmopolitan 'right'. Held agrees that 'the cosmopolitan model requires, as a transitional measure, that the UN system actually live up to its charter'.[57] This requires, in particular, the implementation of the various conventions on human rights and also the enforcement of 'the prohibition on the discretionary right to use force'.[58]

Mary Kaldor, on the other hand, distinguishes between what she refers to as 'cosmopolitanism from above', which 'is to be found in the growing myriad of international organizations', and 'cosmopolitanism from below', arising out of civil society, and more specifically what has come to be known as global or transnational civil society in the form of 'new social movements' and nongovernmental organisations, for example.[59] Civil society represents the political space available for autonomous organisations between the individual (as citizen) and the state (as a sovereign political entity).

According to Kaldor, 'the concept of transnational civil society ... is used to refer to self-organized groups which are non-governmental'. Furthermore, such 'self-organized groups ... represent, in effect, a public pressure for cosmopolitan right'.[60] Global civil society thus provides a normative and institutional basis for cosmopolitanism that is distinct from the state and conventional state sovereignty.

We can see, then, that there is a convergence between cosmopolitanism as an ethical or moral philosophy and internationalism as a political theory, with its commitment to multilateralism and the rule of law at the international level. There is a similar convergence between communitarianism, with its focus upon the primacy of exclusive moral communities, and political realism, with its emphasis upon the irreducible and incommensurable differences between sovereign states as the cornerstone of the international system. Also, the communitarian emphasis on the moral primacy of group solidarity resembles perhaps Niebuhr's 'double morality', with its connection to the realist tradition in international politics.

In the context of this nexus between communitarianism and realism, the state is the ultimate form of moral community. This is related to the argument that in the modern political system citizenship is 'an important component of individuality', with citizenship being a function of state sovereignty. In other words, individualism, supposedly one of three principles of cosmopolitanism as a political theory, derives at least some of its content from the state.[61]

Kant's notion of cosmopolitan right, on the other hand, does suggest that cosmopolitanism can somehow transcend or move beyond internationalism, with its ultimate acceptance of the sovereign state as the fundamental form of political community (even if ostensibly governable by the rule of law). Hedley Bull (interpreting Martin Wight) claims, for example, that for those in the Kantian tradition of international relations theory, international politics was ultimately 'about relations among the human beings of which states were composed' rather than about international or inter-state relations as such.[62]

Thus, cosmopolitanism represents an ontological and not merely an ethical or political challenge to conventional state-centred international theory, whether realist or internationalist. The individualism that is one of the three core principles of cosmopolitanism is metaphysical and not merely ethical. It implies (contrary to communitarianism) that individuals are ontologically prior to states, even in the context of international politics. David Held reiterates the instrumental value of the state concerning the wellbeing of human individuals, as distinct from its ontological status. 'States can be conceived as vehicles to aid the delivery of effective public regulation, equal liberty and social justice, but they should not be thought of as ontologically privileged.'[63]

This ontological individualism also forms the basis of the universalism of cosmopolitanism, which transcends arbitrary or accidental political or cultural boundaries. Individual human beings are the fundamental constituents of international society, which is also 'a society of the whole human race', and for which state and other borders are at best contingent factors.[64]

'For the Kantian ... states, with their supposed finality, are only aggregates of human beings.' The Westphalian state, although it currently dominates the international system, is a product of history and of human agency in the same way that other forms of political organisation have been. 'The state today is no more final than the city-state or a feudal principality.'[65] The state, as both idea and institution, is historically, politically, ethically and ontologically contingent in a way that individual human beings are not.

All this suggests a highly ambitious political project associated with cosmopolitanism, based on its distinctive characteristics as an ethical and a political theory, and applied to the contemporary international political situation. This is sometimes referred to as 'cosmopolitan democracy', and involves at a minimum transcending or superseding state sovereignty as the central principle of both domestic and international politics.

Daniele Archibugi, for example, refers to 'different, overlapping, levels of governance: local, state-wide, inter-state, regional, and global'.[66] Furthermore, 'the concept of sovereignty' is to be replaced 'with that of constitutionalism', so that conflicts between 'the different levels of governance must ... be referred to jurisdictional bodies'.[67] Cosmopolitan governance limits state sovereignty without itself requiring or constituting a state, however.[68] Archibugi refers to the European Union as the 'first international organization which begins to resemble the cosmopolitan model'.[69]

Replacing sovereignty with constitutionalism does not require the creation of a super-state in the form of a world government because 'it rests on the assumption that norms can be respected even in absence [sic] of a coercive power of last resort'.[70] How this is to be achieved is the crucial question, but it does seem to rely ultimately on the capacity of human beings as autonomous moral agents to establish and maintain political and social institutions that reflect and respect their moral status.

David Held, on the other hand, refers to the 'establishment of an effective, accountable, international police/military force for the last-resort use of coercive power in defence of cosmopolitan law' as one of the 'institutional requirements of political cosmopolitanism'.[71] It is difficult to see how such an enforcement capacity could be effective, however, unless it is linked to some sort of transnational (or 'cosmopolitan') political institution with a constitutional status greater than that of an inter-governmental organisation.

In political terms, then, cosmopolitanism is 'an ambitious project whose aim is to achieve a world order based on the rule of law and democracy'.[72] Nonetheless, Hans Küng, for example, argues that this political project cannot succeed without a cosmopolitan or world ethic: 'a better world order cannot be created or even ... enforced with laws, conventions and ordinances alone ... law has no permanent existence without ethics, so there will be *no new world order without a world ethic*'.[73]

The basis for such a world ethic, according to Küng, is an appeal to 'an ethical minimum common to all religions, cultures, civilisations' rather than to consequences, reason, natural law or human rights.[74] In other words, Küng appeals to a world ethic rooted in shared features of existing moral communities and traditions rather than the abstract universalism of cosmopolitan ethical theories. In this, his approach resembles communitarianism except that he argues that moral traditions are not self-contained or exclusive but instead share sufficient values to form the basis of a global ethic. 'Despite all the differences between cultures, there are some themes which appear in almost all cultural traditions and which could serve as the inspiration for a global ethic.'[75] This is particularly true of religions around the world, which he claims agree on such values as 'non-violence and respect for life', for example.[76]

## IV. COSMOPOLITAN RESTRAINTS ON WAR AND ARMED CONFLICT

The community or national loyalties required by war and armed conflict present perhaps the paradigmatic challenge to cosmopolitan ethics. As Erskine suggests: 'The claim to a realm of morality that reaches beyond the boundaries of any particular community is arduously tested by the reality of war.'[77] Whether the armed conflict is about access to resources, control over territory or reinforcing identity (or some combination of these factors), it depends on and exacerbates division between the groups, communities or countries in conflict. It is difficult to maintain or develop a sense of common or shared humanity with the 'enemy' in the context of armed conflict.

Nonetheless, some of the crucial just war principles 'of restraint in the conduct of war' depend on an acceptance or acknowledgement of a cosmopolitan approach. Erskine mentions the *jus in bello* 'norm of "non-combatant immunity", or "discrimination", according to which civilians are not to be intentional targets of organised violence. Such a prohibition epitomises an ethical cosmopolitan perspective: the enemy must be granted moral standing, even in the midst of violent conflict.'[78] The shared humanity of civilians takes precedence over their membership of opposing groups or communities, and their fundamental rights (including the right to life) and dignity must be respected and protected on that basis.

Erskine distinguishes between 'impartialist' and 'embedded' forms of cosmopolitanism. Impartialist cosmopolitanism conforms to the conventional interpretation of cosmopolitanism, in that it requires the impartial application of universal moral principles, abstracted 'from particular ties and loyalties'.[79] Embedded cosmopolitanism, on the other hand, argues that this insistence on 'the moral irrelevance of the deeply entrenched communities that constitute the moral agent' is unrepresentative of our moral experience.[80]

Embedded cosmopolitanism holds, instead, that every moral agent 'is defined by her membership within a web of multiple, multifarious, over-lapping and often non-territorially defined communities'.[81] This multiple community membership more accurately reflects the context within which moral agents make ethical choices than the disembodied and dislocated impartiality of conventional cosmopolitanism. It nonetheless allows each moral agent to transcend the circumscribed or parochial vantage point determined by membership in a unique and exclusive moral community, as suggested by conventional communitarianism.[82]

It does not imply, for example, that the boundaries of the nation-state of which one happens to be a member define or limit the extent of one's moral concerns in the context of international politics, as implied by the position Erskine refers to as 'communitarian realism'.[83] The moral communities to which one belongs are not defined exclusively or even primarily in territorial or political terms.[84]

Erskine argues that these multiple and overlapping community memberships constitutive of every moral agent provide a basis for cosmopolitan principles of restraint during war and armed conflict, such as discrimination or noncombatant immunity, that do not depend on unrealisable commitments to abstract universalism.

> From an embedded cosmopolitan perspective, restraint can be inspired only by a shared membership within a particular community … In response to the enemy, the radically situated self of an embedded cosmopolitan perspective must realise both that she is constituted by multifarious, overlapping and often permeable morally constitutive communities and that the other with whom she is faced is similarly defined by particular memberships that overlap with her own.[85]

In other words, the moral status of civilians is not limited to their membership of an enemy community or country. Instead, they merit respect and protection on the basis of shared membership in some other morally relevant community, and not merely in virtue of an abstract and universal humanity.

Dower also refers to membership in disparate communities in terms of 'divided loyalties', and suggests that such divided loyalties are among the conditions of peace. He distinguishes between loyalty to one's country, for example, and 'to other groups' such as one's church and so on. He argues that such disparate loyalties, presumably of equal value, act somehow as a disincentive to war and violence. 'One is less likely to go to war in response to one of one's loyalties if this means fighting members of other groups one has loyalty to.'[86]

Dower goes further than Erskine, however, in suggesting that we can also have 'loyalty as global citizens to the global community itself'. It is not clear, however, how one is supposed to reconcile conflicting loyalties, in particular one's loyalty to 'the global community itself', and other more specific allegiances. Global citizenship in this sense would seem to be of a different order than other more particular affinities, although Dower does not suggest it should somehow necessarily take priority.[87]

Erskine refers only obliquely to examples of the communities relevant to an embedded cosmopolitan perspective. Such communities seem to correspond to the organisations of civil society, or the autonomous space between the state and the individual, although Erskine does not identify them as such, like trade unions, social welfare groups or political associations of various types.[88] What is not made clear is why membership of such organisations is either constitutive of the moral agent, or morally relevant to the choices they make.

Furthermore, Erskine herself recognises a fundamental difficulty with such an embedded cosmopolitan defence of moral restraint during wartime. 'The problem that remains is that, in some circumstances, there is a paucity of readily apparent communities that would tie the moral agent to either the distant or enemy civilian.'[89] Also, even where common morally relevant communities may exist, combatants may just as easily emphasise community memberships that are in conflict over those that are shared. The moral limits of community became obvious during the 1994 genocide in Rwanda, for example, and during other armed conflicts incorporating issues of identity such as those in the Balkans throughout the 1990s.

These difficulties reveal that so-called embedded cosmopolitanism is a form of communitarianism, involving an expanded sense of what counts as a morally relevant community, rather than a type of cosmopolitanism, with its view that only our common humanity rather than community membership, however broadly defined, is ultimately relevant to moral decision-making. It is for this reason that, as Erskine finally acknowledges, it cannot guarantee principles requiring moral restraint during war and armed conflict that depend on the universality and impartiality implicit in any genuine form of cosmopolitanism.[90]

Both consequentialism and deontology, as rival cosmopolitan theories of normative ethics, contribute principles of moral restraint during war and armed conflict via some of the central criteria of just war theory. Deontological ethics can be seen as a cosmopolitan source or support for the principle of noncombatant immunity, for example. Consequentialism, on the other hand, contributes the principle of proportionality.[91] Noncombatant immunity is a *jus in bello* principle, concerning the conduct of armed groups engaged in war, while proportionality is also a *jus ad bellum* criterion applicable to the initial decision to use military force.

The principle of noncombatant immunity can be deontological if its ban on the intentional targeting of civilians during armed conflict is absolute, and is not contingent on calculations concerning the projected outcome of the war or of a particular military action. It could also be derived from rule-utilitarianism as a particular type of consequentialism, however.

Proportionality, on the other hand, involves an explicitly consequentialist calculation of the expected benefits to be obtained through military action compared to its costs or destructive consequences. Proportionality, furthermore, provides an important qualification to the principle of double effect, which in turn qualifies noncombatant immunity. Unintended civilian casualties are permitted, in other words, but only so long as they do not outweigh the benefits obtained (or at least the harm precluded) by a particular military action.

Furthermore, more recent interpretations of just cause as humanitarian intervention might be linked to a human rights-based cosmopolitan approach to ethics in international politics. Such intervention involves action inside the territorial boundaries of a state, without its consent, in order (ostensibly) to protect the fundamental human rights of its citizens. Bohman and Lutz-Bachman suggest, for example: 'If there is any room for coercion in cosmopolitan law, it is in the enforcement of human rights precisely against states that use their sovereignty to abuse human rights.'[92] Such a cosmopolitan interpretation of humanitarian intervention reiterates the cosmopolitan challenge to the centrality of state sovereignty in conventional international relations theory.

Finally, the cosmopolitan obligation of nonmaleficence, or our perfect or nonoptional duty, as members of the universal moral community, not to harm one another can be linked to a pacifist prohibition against killing more generally that goes beyond noncombatant immunity or the just war principle of discrimination. Thus, both pacifism and just war theory can be compatible with cosmopolitanism as a meta-ethical theory, and the debate between them must also incorporate discussions about specific normative theories as well as the dilemmas offered by particular situations of moral choice in the context of war and armed conflict.

Situations of war and armed conflict provide perhaps the severest test of the cosmopolitan approach to ethics in international politics, because of the dichotomy between the national or community loyalties they inspire and the humanitarian principles supporting moral restraint during violent conflict. 'Embedded cosmopolitanism' is an attempt to overcome this dichotomy by avoiding the abstract and disembodied humanitarianism implied in such principles through grounding them in an expanded nonterritorial sense of community. Even this expanded view of community is insufficient to support the universality and impartiality required by effective cosmopolitan principles of war and peace, however. Instead, existing principles of moral restraint during war and armed conflict, provided by just war criteria for example, can be derived from conventional cosmopolitan normative theories such as deontology and consequentialism. The debate between pacifism and just war theory, on the other hand, cannot be resolved by reference to cosmopolitan principles alone.

# NOTES

1. Cf. Dower, *World Ethics*, p. 23.
2. Held, 'Cosmopolitanism: globalisation tamed?', p. 470.
3. Charvet, 'The Possibility of a Cosmopolitan Ethical Order', p. 523.
4. Cf. Barry, 'International Society from a Cosmopolitan Perspective', p. 144.
5. Beitz, 'Social and Cosmopolitan Liberalism', p. 519.
6. Held, 'Cosmopolitanism: globalisation tamed?', p. 470.
7. Buchanan and Keohane, 'The Preventive Use of Force', p. 1.
8. Dower, *World Ethics*, p. 23.
9. Ibid. p. 102.
10. Erskine, 'Embedded Cosmopolitanism and the Case of War', p. 572.
11. Ibid. pp. 574, 572.
12. Erskine, '"Citizen of nowhere" or "the point where circles intersect"?', p. 477.
13. Carr, *The Twenty Years' Crisis 1919–1939*, pp. 22–3.
14. Ibid. p. 40.
15. Erskine, '"Citizen of nowhere" or "the point where circles intersect"?', p. 462.
16. Ibid. p. 471.
17. John Rawls writes, in *A Theory of Justice*, that consequentialism and deontology can be distinguished in terms of the way they connect the two central concepts of ethics, the right and the good. For consequentialism, right action 'is defined as that which maximises the good'. For deontology, on the other hand, the right is not dependent on the good, since other criteria, such as promise-keeping or truth-telling, may be relevant to deciding our actual duties or obligations, independently of the consequences of conforming to them. See *A Theory of Justice*, p. 24.
18. Dower, *World Ethics*, p. 23.
19. Nussbaum, 'Kant and Cosmopolitanism', p. 30.
20. Honneth, 'Is Universalism a Moral Trap?', p. 167.
21. Linklater, 'The problem of harm in world politics', p. 324 (footnote 18).
22. Nussbaum, 'Kant and Cosmopolitanism', p. 36.
23. Franke, 'Immanuel Kant and the (Im)Possibility of International Relations Theory', p. 296.
24. Held, 'Cosmopolitanism: globalisation tamed?', p. 471.
25. Ibid. p. 473.
26. Kant, 'To Perpetual Peace', p. 119.
27. Franke, 'Immanuel Kant and the (Im)Possibility of International Relations Theory', p. 303.
28. Brown, *International Relations Theory*, pp. 31–3.
29. Ibid., p. 205.
30. Shapcott, 'Cosmopolitan Conversations', p. 225. Shapcott himself is highly critical of the cosmopolitan credentials of discourse ethics.
31. Ibid. p. 227.
32. Brown, *International Relations Theory*, p. 5.
33. Dower, *World Ethics*, p. 86.
34. Ibid. p. 79.
35. Held, 'Cosmopolitanism: globalisation tamed?', p. 474.
36. Kant, 'To Perpetual Peace', p. 107.
37. Beetham, 'Human Rights as a Model for Cosmopolitan Democracy', p. 59.
38. Dower, *World Ethics*, p. 79. Charvet also discusses the distinction between rights defined through membership of 'a particular community and of occupying a

particular position within it', or 'positional rights', and universal or 'genuine' human rights. See Charvet, 'The Possibility of a Cosmopolitan Ethical Order', p. 537.

39. Brown, *International Relations Theory*, p. 24.
40. Cochran, *Normative Theory in International Relations*, p. 9.
41. Brown, *International Relations Theory*, p. 62.
42. Dower, *World Ethics*, p. 20.
43. Erskine, 'Embedded Cosmopolitanism and the Case of War', p. 574.
44. Nussbaum, 'Kant and Cosmopolitanism', p. 31.
45. Erskine, '"Citizen of nowhere" or "the point where circles intersect"?', p. 457.
46. Franke, 'Immanuel Kant and the (Im)Possibility of International Relations Theory', p. 307.
47. Archibugi, 'Principles of Cosmopolitan Democracy', p. 204.
48. Bohman and Lutz-Bachman, 'Introduction', p. 18.
49. Habermas, 'Kant's Idea of Perpetual Peace', p. 128. See also Stevenson, 'Cosmopolitanism and the Future of Democracy', p. 256.
50. Held, 'Cosmopolitanism: globalisation tamed?', p. 474.
51. Dower, *World Ethics*, p. 81.
52. Wight, *International Theory*, pp. 73–4.
53. Bohman and Lutz-Bachman, 'Introduction', p. 14.
54. Habermas, 'Kant's Idea of Perpetual Peace', p. 146.
55. Held, 'Cosmopolitanism: globalisation tamed?', p. 478.
56. Habermas, 'Kant's Idea of Perpetual Peace', p. 126.
57. Held, 'Cosmopolitan Democracy and the Global Order', p. 246.
58. Held, 'Cosmopolitanism: globalisation tamed?', p. 475.
59. Kaldor, *New and Old Wars*, p. 68.
60. Kaldor, 'Introduction', p. 23.
61. Frost, *Ethics in International Relations*, p. 188.
62. Bull, 'Martin Wight and the theory of international relations', p. xii.
63. Held, 'Cosmopolitanism: globalisation tamed?, p. 470.
64. Wight, *International Theory*, p. 36.
65. Ibid. p. 140.
66. Archibugi, 'Cosmopolitan Democracy', p. 6.
67. Ibid. p. 8.
68. Archibugi, 'Principles of Cosmopolitan Democracy', p. 216.
69. Ibid. p. 219.
70. Archibugi, 'Cosmopolitan Democracy', p. 8.
71. Held, 'Cosmopolitanism: globalisation tamed?', p. 478.
72. Archibugi, 'Principles of Cosmopolitan Democracy', p. 198.
73. Küng, 'A Global Ethic for a New Global Order', p. 142 (emphasis in original).
74. Ibid. p. 134.
75. Ibid. p. 137.
76. Ibid. p. 144.
77. Erskine, 'Embedded Cosmopolitanism and the Case of War', p. 570.
78. Ibid. p. 570.
79. Ibid. p. 574.
80. Ibid. p. 582.
81. Ibid. p. 575.
82. Ibid. p. 576.
83. Ibid. p. 573.
84. Cf. Erskine's critique of 'communitarian realism', ibid. p. 582.

85. Ibid. p. 588.
86. Dower, 'Global Citizenship and Peace', p. 251.
87. Ibid. p. 251.
88. Erskine, 'Embedded Cosmopolitanism and the Case of War', p. 575.
89. Ibid. p. 589.
90. Ibid. p. 590.
91. Dower, *World Ethics*, pp. 78–9.
92. Bohman and Lutz-Bachman, 'Introduction', p. 18.

# PART II

# ETHICAL APPROACHES TO PEACE AND WAR

# CHAPTER 5

# JUST WAR AND THE STATE

Just war theory represents perhaps the most venerable and coherent attempt to develop a comprehensive set of moral constraints on the use of armed force, using ethical criteria to assess both the decision to go to war (*jus ad bellum*) and the methods used to achieve its aims (*jus in bello*). In this sense, as Coates points out, just war theory assumes that war is 'a rule-governed, institutional activity, and not a condition of utter lawlessness in which all legal and moral constraints cease to apply'.[1]

This suggests that the international system as a whole is also institutionalised and rule-governed, and that sometimes these rules need to be enforced. Thus, one function of just war theory is to provide the conditions under which armed force may be used to defend and maintain the rules of the international system.

Just war theory, therefore, seeks both to limit or constrain the use of armed force and to justify its use. In other words, the limits placed on the use of armed force by just war theory are determined by the role of force in maintaining and defending the rules of the international system.

These rules, such as national sovereignty and noninterference in the internal affairs of other countries, tend to be based on the central role of the state. Similarly, current interpretations of just war criteria also tend to focus on the primacy of the state, as the modern form of sovereign political authority. This is reflected in the *jus ad bellum* criteria of legitimate authority, just cause as self-defence against aggression, and last resort, with its emphasis on diplomacy as an alternative to war. It even appears in the *jus in bello* criterion of noncombatant immunity, in the sense that combatant/noncombatant roles are state-defined, so that soldiers, as armed agents of the state, become legitimate military targets regardless of their personal moral culpability. Thus, from a cosmopolitan and pacifist perspective, the ambivalence of just war theory towards the use of armed force combined with its focus on the state (or at least centralised political authority) circumscribes its ability to transform international politics and contribute towards the elimination of war.

## I. JUST WAR CRITERIA

Just war theory consists of two distinct parts, each containing criteria concerning the moral permissibility of war. These are *jus ad bellum*, which regulates the ends or goals of war, and *jus in bello*, which regulates its means, or the methods used to achieve these goals.

There are six standard *jus ad bellum* criteria, and two standard *jus in bello* criteria. The six standard *jus ad bellum* criteria are: legitimate authority, just cause, last resort, proportionality, right intention and probable success. The two standard *jus in bello* criteria are proportionality and noncombatant immunity.

According to just war theory, the decision to go to war must be made by a competent or legitimate authority. In the modern era this is usually taken to mean a state, as a sovereign political entity, because the modern state is defined in terms of having a monopoly over the legitimate use of force or violence, both externally and internally. As Dower writes, 'ever since the development of the modern nation-state system, it has been a key feature of its rationale that nation-states are the units, and no others are, who can legitimately use organised violence in pursuit of their ends'.[2]

Under Article 42 of the UN Charter, however, the UN Security Council has become the sole legitimate authority for authorising the use of armed force 'to maintain or restore international peace and security'. This rules out the unilateral use of armed force or war as an instrument of any state's foreign policy.

Otherwise, the use of armed force is restricted to the immediate self-defence of member-states 'if an armed attack occurs', in accordance with Article 51. This is connected to the second *jus ad bellum* criterion, just cause, which in modern times has been defined in terms of defence of a country or state against armed aggression.

War must also be a last resort, all available peaceful means having failed. The criterion of proportionality is applied to the war as a whole. In other words, the benefits resulting from the war, or at least the harm it prevents, must outweigh the harm it causes.

The criterion of right intention is sometimes taken to be a refinement of just cause, so that not merely must there be a just cause for going to war, but the war must be fought for this reason. Similarly, the sixth criterion, reasonable hope of success for producing the good (as opposed to the harm) resulting from the war, adds probability considerations to those of proportionality.

As well as these *jus ad bellum* criteria, concerning the decision to go to war, or the reasons for which a war is fought, there are also two *jus in bello* criteria, governing the way in which it is fought. The criterion of proportionality, concerning beneficial and harmful results, must be applied to particular military actions, as well as to the war as a whole. The principle of discrimination, or noncombatant immunity, requires that civilians, as noncombatants, must not be deliberately attacked or killed at any time. Noncombatants must never be directly targeted by military activity.[3] 'The fighting must be directed solely against the armed forces of the enemy.'[4]

Both sets of criteria, *jus ad bello* and *jus in bellum*, provide strict requirements that any war must fulfil if it is to be morally justified or permissible. Furthermore, all of these requirements must be met. None of them is optional, and none takes priority or makes any of the others redundant.

A. J. Coates argues quite vehemently that a just cause, for example, 'is a necessary but not a sufficient condition of just recourse' to war, or *jus ad bellum*. Other criteria, such as proportionality, last resort and probable success, must also be satisfied. Thus, he writes that 'even when the cause is most certainly just it may not be serious or weighty enough to warrant such a drastic remedy as war; or there may be other means of redress short of war that have not been tried or exhausted; or the prospects of success may be so remote as to rule war out'. Furthermore, 'however just the recourse to war, combatants are not excused from the moral constraints that apply to the conduct of war', or *jus in bello* requirements.[5]

Dower does, however, raise the issue as to whether all just war conditions must be met, or merely a sufficient number of them.[6] Then, however, we could ask which of the criteria could be overruled for a war to maintain its 'justness'. In the case of NATO's military campaign against Serbia in 1999, for example, NATO claimed 'just cause' in support of its action, without fulfilling the criterion of 'legitimate authority' in the form of a UN Security Council resolution.

## II. JUS AD BELLUM

As this example reveals, states often seem to adopt a selective or à la carte approach when they claim to be implementing just war principles. There can also be conflicting or even contradictory interpretations of specific just war criteria. 'Just cause', according to Norman, refers to the righting (or prevention) of a specific wrong. Furthermore, it has come to focus increasingly on one particular wrong, 'the crime of aggression', so that the 'just cause' that makes going to war morally permissible is 'defence against aggression'.[7] In the context of the modern state system, any 'use or threat of force by one state against the political sovereignty or territorial integrity of another constitutes aggression'.[8]

Contemporary proponents of just war theory, such as Michael Walzer, often emphasise self-defence as a moral justification for war. The importance of self-defence is justified by the centrality of state sovereignty within the international system, which in turn implies the principle of nonintervention within the internal affairs of sovereign states.[9] A violation of the sovereignty or territorial integrity of a state, or aggression, justifies both 'a war of self-defense by the victim and a war of law enforcement by the victim and any other member of international society'. These two types of war coincide with the only two uses of military force permitted by the UN Charter (under Articles 42 and 51), which otherwise prohibits its use in international affairs (Article 2(4)), although Walzer himself does not make this connection. Furthermore, only self-defence against aggression 'can justify war', since the 'central purpose of the theory is to limit the occasions for war'.[10] Self-defence against aggression, or the 'defense of rights', is the only justifiable reason for going to war. What Walzer refers to as the 'legalist paradigm', or his 'theory of aggression', 'rules out every other sort of war'.[11]

David Rodin has presented a forceful critique of the analogy between individual and national self-defence, which he claims provides the ethical or philosophical basis for self-defence as just cause.[12] Ian Holliday, on the other hand, suggests that this focus on self-defence as just cause is 'too limiting'. Instead, he argues for 'a theory premised on justice', because 'the obvious candidate [for just cause] is its precise opposite, namely demonstrable injustice. Naturally, this does not exclude self-defence, for unprovoked attack is demonstrably unjust.'[13] In other words, the rectification of 'demonstrable injustice' (which includes but is much broader than the crime of aggression) becomes the 'just cause' for which war can be fought.

E. H. Carr had already queried self-defence as the sole moral justification for war. 'The moral criterion must be not the "aggressive" or "defensive" character of the war, but the nature of the change which is being sought and resisted.' In other words, there may be situations in which 'the use or threatened use of force to maintain the *status quo* may be morally more culpable than the use or threatened use of force to alter it',[14] where the status quo is a manifestly unjust or repressive government, for instance. Walzer himself also concedes fundamental revisions to his initial formulation of the legalist paradigm governing the use of military force in international affairs that 'open the way for just wars that are not fought in self-defense or against aggression in the strict sense'.[15]

In the last decade, for example, the practice of international humanitarian intervention has been used to supplement self-defence as a 'just cause' in a way that would accord with this expanded definition. One of

Walzer's 'revisions' to the legalist paradigm, for instance, includes military intervention in the internal affairs of a state 'when the violation of human rights within a set of boundaries is so terrible ... that is, in cases of enslavement or massacre'.[16] Thus, NATO's 'just cause' during its military campaign against Serbia in 1999 was the gross human rights abuses being perpetrated against the Albanian population of Kosovo by Serbian military forces.

There is a crucial tension between 'self-defence' and 'humanitarian intervention' as the fulfilment of the just cause criterion, however, because self-defence is aimed at the protection of state sovereignty, whereas humanitarian intervention requires the active and deliberate violation of a state's sovereignty in order to protect the fundamental human rights of those within its jurisdiction. In the case of NATO's bombing campaign against Serbia, for example, NATO might claim just cause in the name of ending massive human rights abuses, while Serbia might claim just cause in the name of self-defence, since the NATO action involved interference in its internal affairs in the absence of a UN mandate.

Also, it is not always easy to define what is meant by or included as defensive (as distinct from aggressive) military action. The first use of weapons may not always be considered an act of aggression, for example, if we allow pre-emptive first strikes to be viewed as defensive actions against immediate threats.[17] Nonetheless, as Coates points out, international law, in the form of the UN Charter, does not support this interpretation of pre-emptive action as a form of self-defence. 'Article 51 of the UN Charter, for example, speaks of "the inherent right of individual or collective self-defence *if an armed attack occurs*".'[18] It would seem that a consistent, transparent and shared interpretation of a just war criterion such as self-defence is crucial to its successful implementation.

The criterion of 'right intention' is sometimes presented as a qualification of the 'just cause' criterion, rather than a *jus ad bellum* criterion in its own right.[19] The purpose of this qualification is to ensure that the 'just cause' is not merely a rhetorical device cloaking the pursuit of self-interest by means of the use of armed force.

This is not to suggest that the intentions must be purely disinterested, as Coates points out.[20] States cannot be expected to behave entirely altruistically or on the basis of moral obligation to others alone. The motives of any state, or at least of its governing elite, will be mixed at best. Right intention, however, is meant to ensure that just war considerations concerning the use of armed force are not superseded or replaced by more self-interested objectives. One test of right intention might be a state's willingness to apply all just war criteria consistently to its use of armed force. The selective use of just war criteria (as in the example of

NATO's bombing campaign against Serbia), on the other hand, is an indication that motives other than a genuine willingness to conform to the requirements of just war theory are at work.

The criterion of 'legitimate authority' is the most obvious example of a state-centred just war principle, even when this authority is elevated to the level of the UN Security Council, since the UN is an organ of its member states. In accordance with conventional Western political theory (especially social contract theory), Coates insists that 'the public monopoly of the use of force', in the form of the state, 'represents a fundamental step in any process of pacification',[21] because it restricts the legitimate use of armed force both domestically and internationally to the state as an agent of law enforcement.

This raises the question as to whether nonstate actors, such as national liberation movements or resistance movements, can claim the right to use armed force. It is the public, or representative, character of the state that is its key feature in terms of establishing its monopoly over the legitimate use of force. Thus, according to Coates, 'the private appropriation of power by the government of a state', or the use of the state apparatus to obtain purely private ends, 'undermines its legitimacy and establishes, at least in principle, the right of resistance'.[22] Even Michael Walzer, who links the state so closely to moral community, concedes: 'The rights of states rest on the consent of their members ... If no common life exists, or if the state doesn't defend the common life that does exist, its own defense may have no moral justification.'[23] A state's legitimacy, in other words, depends on its capacity to defend the rights of the individual citizens or persons it claims to represent.

It could be argued that in the case of apartheid in South Africa, for example, the state was by no means a public or representative body. However, as Coates points out, the resistance itself must be representative in order to fulfil the criterion of legitimacy that is being violated by the ruling regime: 'since it is the private use of force by the ruler or regime against the community that justifies resistance in the first place, the right of resistance is enjoyed only by the community or by its agents or representatives'.[24] Similarly, Holliday suggests that 'we need to insist on a significant measure of popular support for a proposed war-making agency', whether state or nonstate.[25]

In addition to representativeness as an internal criterion of legitimacy concerning the right to go to war, Coates mentions two external criteria for determining this right: 'membership of an international community to the common good of which the state is ordered and to the law of which it is subject'.[26] This requires some effort on the part of states to transcend the unilateral pursuit of narrow self-interest, as well as adherence to the

UN Charter and other international treaties and conventions. Although Coates does not specify this, these criteria could also be applied to non-state actors insofar as they are ordered to the common international good and they can be subject to international law.

This interpretation of 'legitimate authority' permits the use of armed force by nonstate actors, but it is still state-centred because such actors only gain legitimacy insofar as they meet essential criteria of the representative or democratic state. Furthermore, such nonstate actors, such as the ANC in South Africa, are usually aspiring governments, seeking control of state power. Al Qaeda and similar networks are a crucial current exception to this, however, indicating the changing nature of political violence and armed conflict in the new century.

One problem with this view of legitimacy is that it continues to be connected to political authority and mechanisms of social power, that is, the state and the functions of the state. Furthermore, the purpose of legitimacy in this context is to permit the use of armed force, for social and political control, both internally and externally.

'Proportionality' is a consequentialist criterion, requiring some calculation or prediction of the expected outcomes of the use of armed force, in terms of harm or destruction caused versus benefits obtained (or at least harm prevented). Furthermore, such an assessment must be based on the expected impact of war on all those likely to be affected, including uninvolved countries and the enemy as well as the country making the decision about whether or not to go to war.[27]

Also, Gary D. Brown argues that *jus ad bellum* proportionality calculations must continue throughout the course of an armed conflict. As soon as 'the harm that was to be avoided by war has been prevented … the armed action should end', in order to minimise the damage resulting from resort to war. He suggests that US-led action against Iraq following the end of the first Gulf War in 1991 does not conform to this application of the proportionality criterion.[28]

Such a calculation is perhaps more reliable in the context of proportionality as a *jus in bello* criterion, concerning specific military actions, as distinct from proportionality as a *jus ad bellum* criterion, applied to a war or military campaign as a whole. Coates, for example, suggests that proportionality 'should be "proximate" rather than remote in its moral application',[29] to maximise its reliability. It becomes difficult, then, to justify distant or long-term benefits in comparison to the immediate harm and destruction resulting from the use of armed force. Even so, Laurie Calhoun suggests 'a sober assessment of the long-range consequences of recourse to military measures reveals that they are unlikely ever to maximise utility'.[30] If we accept both sets of arguments, concerning long-

term as well as proximate or immediate consequences of the use of
force, it becomes difficult to see how proportionality could ever be
fied as a *jus ad bellum* criterion in accordance with consequent
calculations.

Coates' point concerning proximate consequences is connected
probability considerations, or 'reasonable hope for success', since the more
remote an anticipated outcome, the more difficult it is to expect or predict
its attainment. It is for this reason that probability, or reasonable hope for
success, is sometimes considered a qualification of proportionality, rather
than a criterion in its own right.[31] In other words, the proportionality
criterion gives more weight to those predicted consequences that are more
immediate and hence more likely to occur. Holliday refers to the combination of these two criteria as a 'risk assessment exercise' that involves
'weighing contingent factors'.[32]

The criterion of 'last resort' perhaps encapsulates just war theory's
moral presumption against war most clearly, since it requires that all
peaceful means to right the wrong of the 'just cause' criterion must have
been exhausted before the use of armed force can be justified.[33] Thus, 'we
need to be clear that there exists in the world a problem to which war is the
only viable solution'.[34]

The 'last resort' criterion includes both a practical and a moral component. The practical component concerns the effectiveness of peaceful
means, such as diplomatic pressure, in righting the wrong. As Coates
suggests: 'In relation to the criterion of last resort … instrumental power
… is a major concern, since what the principle enjoins is the exhaustion of
*effective* alternatives to war.'[35] For 'the alternative defence strategies of
non-violent resistance'[36] to preclude the use of military force against armed
aggression, for example, they must demonstrate their effectiveness.

The moral component concerns whether or not the so-called peaceful
means, such as economic sanctions, are more or less destructive than the
use of armed force. As Coates argues:

> a blockade may constitute a grosser violation of morality than war itself,
> involving as it does a systematic attack on the civilian or noncombatant sections
> of the community … In some important respects there seems little to choose
> between the blockade and strategic bombing, to which historically it is related:
> both prefer an attack on the sources of supply and civilian morale to an
> engagement with enemy forces, and both are for that very reason morally
> problematic.[37]

Last resort requires alternatives to the use of armed force that are not
only effective, but also moral, in the sense that they do not violate other
just war criteria, such as proportionality and noncombatant immunity.

## III. JUS IN BELLO

The *jus in bello* principle of discrimination, or noncombatant immunity, also raises moral and practical difficulties for just war theory. In practical terms, of course, it is almost impossible to wage a war in which there are no civilian casualties, or in which civilian casualties are completely avoided. Even the most sophisticated of precision weapons cannot eliminate civilian casualties, as the recent wars against Afghanistan and Iraq (including the Gulf War of 1991) have demonstrated, due to human error, systems failure and so on.[38] For this reason, the criterion of non-combatant immunity is often qualified by the principle of double effect in order to overcome this difficulty for just war theory.

The essential feature of the principle of double effect is that the death or injury of innocents in war is morally excusable if this is not the intended consequence of an act of war, but merely its unfortunate by-product (that is, 'collateral damage'). In other words, the deliberate targeting of civilians in war remains prohibited, but unplanned or unintended civilian casualties do not disallow a military action in moral terms according to this principle. Furthermore, just as noncombatant casualties cannot be intended as an outcome of military action in their own right, they cannot be sought as a means to some other military objective[39] (such as undermining the enemy's morale or will to fight).

There are at least two further qualifications to this principle, provided by other just war criteria. Firstly, the intended effect of the military action must itself be justifiable in just war terms, that is, it must be aimed at pursuing a 'just cause'. Secondly, the good of achieving the intended effect must outweigh 'the evil of the unintended, secondary, or collateral effect, the death or injury to innocents'.[40] In other words, the unintended civilian casualties of an act of war are still limited by the criteria of just cause and proportionality.[41]

The principle of discrimination, together with these qualifications, is formulated most closely in international law in Additional Protocol 1 to the 1949 Geneva Conventions. According to Nicholas Wheeler, this 'legal instrument enshrines Just War's absolute prohibition against the deliberate killing of civilians', with the proportionality criterion applied to the '"incidental loss of civilian life, injury to civilians, damage to civilian objects, or a combination thereof"'.[42]

From the perspective of those suffering as a result of military action, of course, the principle of double effect seems remarkably callous and inhumane. As Calhoun points out: 'Apologies for collateral damage are satisfying only to the killers, never to the families, friends and fellow citizens of the victims.'[43]

Partly in response to this difficulty, Walzer suggests that double effect must be strengthened by the principle of 'due care', according to which combatants have a positive responsibility to 'save civilian lives' and reduce the risk of civilian casualties, beyond the minimum requirements of proportionality. 'Whenever there is likely to be a second effect, a second intention is morally required', summed up by this need for 'due care' to be taken. Furthermore, fulfilling this principle may involve additional risks to soldiers' lives, if this minimises the risks to noncombatants.[44] Thus, the NATO bombing campaign against Serbia is sometimes criticised precisely because the 15,000-foot limit on air operations in the name of 'force protection', that is, to reduce the risk to NATO aircrew, unjustifiably increased the risk to Serb civilians on the ground. Wheeler concludes: 'It is entirely reasonable that the armed forces should seek to reduce their risks; the problem arises when this has the effect of imposing additional risks on civilians.'[45]

Whitley Kaufman also suggests that, in accordance with the doctrine of double effect, not only must bad effects (such as civilian casualties) be unintended, but that 'the agent always has the duty to minimize the bad effects'. Furthermore, 'in wartime this means that a combatant must be willing to accept a substantial increase in risk to his own safety in order to protect innocents from the risk of harm; it also requires that one take any possible steps to protect civilians'.[46] In other words, in accordance with this principle of due care, noncombatant casualties become acceptable not merely when they are unintended, but only when they are unavoidable.

The combatant/noncombatant (or civilian) distinction is a descriptive rather than a moral distinction, however. It describes different roles or functions people perform in the context of war, without on its own implying moral judgements concerning those roles or functions. We have to ask the further question as to why this descriptive distinction is morally relevant.

One suggestion is that we need to be interested instead in the distinction between those who are morally responsible (or culpable) and those who are morally innocent of wrongdoing in the context of a war. The problem for the principle of noncombatant immunity of just war theory is that the descriptive distinction between noncombatants (or civilians) and combatants, and the ethical distinction between moral innocence and moral culpability in the context of war, do not necessarily coincide.

There can be civilians, such as politicians or political leaders, whether local or national, who can have more control over (and hence responsibility for) initiating and conducting a war than any of the actual combatants, who may simply be conscripts unaware of who, why or even where they are fighting. Also, as Coates points out, civilians can 'provide the means and instruments of combat'[47] through working in factories producing weapons and munitions, for example. Furthermore, Robert L. Holmes argues: 'If a war is just, the soldier who fights on that side is as innocent as the civilian who stays behind.'[48] So, the principle of non-combatant immunity does not coincide with a genuinely moral distinction between the morally culpable and the morally innocent during wartime, providing 'noncombatant' is taken to be synonymous with 'civilian' and 'combatant' is taken to be synonymous with 'soldier'.

One way of clarifying the remit or applicability of the criterion of noncombatant immunity is to interpret it in terms of 'level of threat' rather than 'moral culpability', in the context of war. Paul Ramsey refers to this as 'objective' or 'functional' innocence rather than moral innocence, as applied to noncombatants.[49]

In this way, any soldier engaged in combat becomes a legitimate target, in accordance with the criterion, because they pose a direct threat to the opposing side, whether or not they are conscripts or volunteers, or fighting for a just or unjust cause. Similarly, civilians can be considered combatants only to the extent that they participate in or directly support an immediate threat posed by the war-making capacity of a state (or other legitimate political entity) engaged in armed conflict. This could apply to factory workers just as much as to political leaders.

Thus, Richard Norman argues that the category of combatant, according to this criterion, 'includes not only soldiers but their military and political leaders, and others who contribute directly to the war effort such as, perhaps, workers in munitions factories. Because they are engaged in an attempt to destroy you, it is permissible to kill them',[50] at least in accordance with this principle. In general, however, because 'noncombatants pose no immediate, imminent threat to life or limb, they are not permissible targets during war'.[51]

Finally, soldiers who have been injured or taken prisoner no longer count as combatants (in accordance with the Geneva Conventions) because they no longer pose a threat to the opposing side. This of course suggests that the descriptive distinction between civilians and soldiers is no longer synonymous with the normative distinction between noncombatants and combatants, for the purposes of applying the principle of discrimination, or noncombatant immunity.

It may be as difficult to establish 'level of threat' as it is to determine 'moral culpability' in the context of war, however, particularly when applied to civilians. Hence, another way to defend the combatant–noncombatant distinction is to rely on political theory to identify soldiers as the armed 'agents of the state' who become permissible targets during war precisely because states are the political entities that can employ armed force legitimately. This limits the cosmopolitan implications of this principle, however, because the moral status of individuals in war becomes defined by their relationship to the state rather than by their membership of a universal moral community.

## IV. LIMITS OF JUST WAR THEORY

Just war theory contains a fundamental moral ambivalence towards war and the use of armed force. On the one hand, it is based on a presumption against war and in favour of peace. Only those instances of armed force that satisfy the exacting requirements of just war theory can be considered exceptions to this general prohibition against war, reflected in Article 2(4) of the UN Charter, for example. As Brown says: 'Exceptional justification is required to cross the threshold of war.'[52] On the other hand, it is precisely through justifying the use of armed force that just war theory can be seen to facilitate and legitimate its continued availability as an instrument of foreign policy.

A. J. Coates suggests that just war theory is a central form of peacemaking, in the sense that it is a vital part of 'the progressive and qualitative improvement or transformation of the international order'[53] aimed ultimately at ridding the world of war. In other words, just war theory, with its strong moral presumption against the use of armed force, aims at eliminating and not merely limiting war.[54] It can achieve this by being part of the transformation of world politics to create the conditions in which war will no longer be necessary, through establishing strong multilateral institutions and the rule of law at the international level. The particular contribution of just war theory can be to provide the normative content or substance of international humanitarian law, for example. Brown agrees that just war theory can contribute to this transformation of international politics. 'If we continue building peaceful problem-solving methods and restricting war-making, then someday war as a method of resolving differences might become rare (and humane even in those few instances).'[55]

Coates acknowledges, however, that for its critics just war theory is not part of the transformation of world politics, but rather a way of justifying the used of armed force as a permanent, even if circumscribed, feature of the international system.

> [T]he tradition ends up sustaining and strengthening the institution of war, its very attempt to subject war to moral regulation lending moral credibility and support to the activity. It has become one of the mainstays of the prevailing system of war, and a prime obstacle to the achievement of a real peace.[56]

In other words, through endeavouring to make war a rule-governed activity, just war theory also serves to institutionalise it rather than remove or eliminate it.

These positions are not entirely exclusive, however. Coates is correct in arguing that the implementation or institutionalisation of just war principles would require the transformation of world politics away from a condition of international anarchy under which moral rules do not apply and are certainly not relevant to the use of military force. It has also been suggested, however, that just war principles follow rather than precede changes to the international system. Thus, the modern emphasis on the defence of national sovereignty as just cause could only occur following the rise of the Westphalian system to replace feudalism in Europe.[57]

In other words, changes to the interpretation of just war principles as a set of normative constraints upon the use of armed force reflect rather than determine the structures of international politics. From an antiwar or antimilitarist perspective, this is perhaps one of the weaknesses of just war theory, because it limits its capacity to provide the normative basis for the elimination of war as a feature of international politics.

Even if the use of armed force could be limited or circumscribed in accordance with just war principles, it is difficult to see why this would lead to the eventual elimination of war. If just war criteria were fully accepted and implemented by the international community, through the mechanisms of international law, for example, the threat of war, at a minimum, would remain a permanent feature of the international system, as a last resort and as a form of immediate self-defence, for example. Rather than eliminating war, in fulfilment of the pacifist dream, the enforcement of just war principles can succeed only in institutionalising it.

Just war theory certainly has cosmopolitan elements, as represented most obviously perhaps by the principle of discrimination, or noncombatant immunity. According to Walzer, for example, in the context of war 'the structure of rights' implied by this principle 'stands independently of political allegiance; it establishes obligations that are owed, so to speak, to humanity itself and to particular human beings and not merely to one's fellow citizens'.[58] In other words, in accordance with this principle soldiers have the same obligations to civilians from an enemy country as they do to civilians from their own (or an allied) country, because of their shared humanity and their shared status as noncombatants.

On the other hand, just war theory is suspect from a cosmopolitan perspective because, in its modern variants at least, it is so strongly state-centric. This is reflected in modern interpretations of the criteria of legitimate authority and just cause in particular.

This state-centrism, in turn, is often rooted in a communitarian rather than a cosmopolitan theory of ethics. This is reflected in Michael Walzer's focus on the defence of national sovereignty as 'just cause' and as the most important *jus ad bellum* criterion, for which he provides deliberately communitarian arguments. He writes, for example, that 'the survival and freedom of political communities – whose members share a way of life, developed by their ancestors to be passed on to their children – are the highest values of international society'.[59] Similarly, he claims that 'the survival and independence of the separate political communities' represented by states represent 'the dominant values' of 'international society'.[60] Coates also suggests that just war theory 'is universalist without being cosmopolitan, and the universal order that it promotes is not without internal variety or differentiation'.[61] The moral priority given to political communities, embodied by the modern nation-state, gives such interpretations of just war theory a distinctly noncosmopolitan ethos.

## NOTES

1. Coates, *The Ethics of War*, p. 114.
2. Dower, *World Ethics*, p. 115.
3. Michael Walzer emphasises the importance of this criterion in his seminal book *Just and Unjust Wars*, p. 15ff.
4. Norman, *Ethics, Killing and War*, p. 119.
5. Coates, *The Ethics of War*, p. 147.
6. Dower, *World Ethics*, pp. 123–4.
7. Norman, *Ethics, Killing and War*, pp. 119–20.
8. Cady, *From Warism to Pacifism*, p. 25. See also Walzer, *Just and Unjust Wars*, p. 62: 'Any use of force or imminent threat of force by one state against the political sovereignty or territorial integrity of another constitutes aggression and is a criminal act.'
9. See Walzer, *Just and Unjust Wars*, p. 51ff.
10. Ibid. p. 62.
11. Ibid. p. 72.
12. See Rodin, *War and Self-Defense*.
13. Holliday, 'Ethics of Intervention', p. 126.
14. Carr, *The Twenty Years' Crisis 1919–1939*, p. 208.
15. Walzer, *Just and Unjust Wars*, p. 90.
16. Ibid. p. 90.
17. See Ibid. p. 80ff.
18. Coates, *The Ethics of War*, p. 159 (emphasis added).
19. Ibid. p. 9.
20. Ibid. p. 162.
21. Ibid. p. 125.
22. Ibid. p. 129.
23. Walzer, *Just and Unjust Wars*, p. 54.
24. Coates, *The Ethics of War*, p. 134.
25. Holliday, 'When is a cause just?', p. 567.
26. Coates, *The Ethics of War*, p. 127.
27. Brown, 'Proportionality and Just War', p. 175.
28. Ibid. pp. 176–7.
29. Coates, *The Ethics of War*, p. 173.

30. Calhoun, 'How Violence Breeds Violence', p. 96.
31. Coates, *The Ethics of War*, p. 9.
32. Holliday, 'Ethics of Intervention', p. 126.
33. Cf. Cady, *From Warism to Pacifism*, p. 26.
34. Holliday, 'Ethics of Intervention', p. 126.
35. Coates, *The Ethics of War*, p. 197.
36. Ibid. p. 115.
37. Ibid. p. 198.
38. Cf. Wheeler, 'Dying for "Enduring Freedom"'.
39. Coates, *The Ethics of War*, p. 245.
40. Cady, *From Warism to Pacifism*, p. 30.
41. See also Kaufman, 'What is the Scope of Civilian Immunity in Wartime?', p. 188 for 'a brief statement of the four provisions of the Doctrine of Double Effect'.
42. Wheeler, 'Dying for "Enduring Freedom"', pp. 208–9.
43. Calhoun, 'How Violence Breeds Violence', p. 98.
44. Walzer, *Just and Unjust Wars*, p. 156.
45. Wheeler, 'Dying for "Enduring Freedom"', p. 220.
46. Kaufman, 'What is the Scope of Civilian Immunity in Wartime?', pp. 193–4.
47. Coates, *The Ethics of War*, p. 237.
48. Holmes, *On War and Morality*, p. 186.
49. Cf. Kaufman, 'What is the Scope of Civilian Immunity in Wartime?', p. 193.
50. Norman, 'The Case for Pacifism', pp. 174–5.
51. Kaufman, 'What is the Scope of Civilian Immunity in Wartime?', p. 188.
52. Brown, 'Proportionality and Just War', p. 173.
53. Coates, *The Ethics of War*, p. 279.
54. Ibid. p. 291.
55. Brown, 'Proportionality and Just War', p. 184.
56. Coates, *The Ethics of War*, p. 4.
57. Müllerson, '*Jus Ad Bellum*', p. 152.
58. Walzer, *Just and Unjust Wars*, p. 158.
59. Ibid. p. 254.
60. Ibid. p. 61.
61. Coates, *The Ethics of War*, p. 7.

CHAPTER 6

# THE POLITICS OF
# PACIFISM

Pacifism is conventionally presented as the view that it is morally wrong to support or participate in war. As A. J. Coates writes, '"pacifism" stands for "the moral renunciation of war". It is the *moral* renunciation of war that is in question.'[1] Pacifists oppose the use of armed force both internationally (war), as well as domestically to achieve social and political change (violent revolution).

As such, pacifism is essentially an ethical position, and requires a political theory to support its principled opposition to war and the use of armed force. Cosmopolitanism may provide pacifism with the theory of international relations it needs, although cosmopolitanism itself does not imply a pacifist response to war.

In political terms, we can distinguish between the reformist and revolutionary implications of pacifism. Reformist pacifism looks for alternative, nonviolent mechanisms for defending conventional political institutions such as the nation-state. Revolutionary pacifism, on the other hand, seeks to transcend or replace such political structures precisely because they depend upon the use of war and armed force as their ultimate sanction. It is this latter form of revolutionary pacifism that coincides most closely with cosmopolitanism as a theory of international politics, because it values human beings as part of a shared moral community above particular political institutions, which have a purely instrumental value at best.

## I. VARIETIES OF PACIFISM

As an ethical position, pacifism has both religious and secular sources. In terms of its influence over the last century or so, it has two main religious sources: 'Hindu philosophy and the example of Gandhi', and individual Christians (such as Tolstoy) or Christian sects (such as the Quakers)[2] that stress 'the perfectionist teachings of the New Testament'.[3]

The modern secular case against war has its roots in the Enlightenment.

The men of the Enlightenment attacked war as both inhumane and irrational ...
They denounced war, too, as in total contradiction to their ideal of human
brotherhood and unity.[4]

Its secular intellectual origins in the Enlightenment may help us connect
the moral condemnation of war expressed through pacifism with cosmopolitanism as a political theory.

Martin Ceadel outlines five types of pacifism in his book *Thinking
about Peace and War*: force (or violence) pacifism, killing pacifism, war
pacifism, modern war pacifism, and nuclear era pacifism.[5] Each of these
five types is defined by the particular moral problem or issue with which
it is concerned, from force or violence through to the use of nuclear
weapons. Furthermore, each subsequent type of pacifism in the list is a
subset of previous types in the list, so that (for example) killing pacifism
is a particular type of violence pacifism, and nuclear era pacifism is a type
of modern war pacifism.

Modern or nuclear era war involves particular reasons for opposing
war for some pacifists because of the degree of destructiveness associated
with either modern weapons in general or nuclear weapons in particular.
'Some pacifists profess an objection not to war as such but only to modern
war: they argue that just wars were once possible but are no longer so in
view of the indiscriminate destructiveness of modern technology.' Bertrand Russell, for example, wrote in 1936 that his pacifism 'depends on the
destructiveness of air power,' that is, mass aerial bombing.[6]

Russell denied that he was 'a complete pacifist', because he always
held 'that some wars have been justified and others not'.[7] Nonetheless,
'while not taking the extreme Tolstoyan view that war is under all circumstances a crime',[8] he also held that the destructive capabilities of the
modern weapons of war meant that 'war cannot still be used as an instrument of policy'.[9] In this sense, it is fair to characterise Russell's position
as that of a 'modern war' pacifist.

Duane L. Cady refers to this as 'technological pacifism' because 'the
means of war in modern technological society have put the possibility of
war behind us'.[10] He suggests, furthermore, that 'the most common
version of this stage on our continuum can be called nuclear pacifism' and
that this can equally extend to concerns about biological and chemical
weapons.[11]

For nuclear era pacifists, moral objections to the use of nuclear
weapons involve a 'more widespread opposition to war through a process
of linkage'. During the Cold War in particular, 'the perceived danger that
a conventional war might develop into a nuclear war ... was thought sufficient to rule out just recourse to conventional arms ... even though
conventional war itself was not regarded as intrinsically immoral'.[12]

Russell, for example, claimed that: 'Whatever agreements not to use hydrogen bombs had been reached in time of peace, they would no longer be considered binding in time of war.'[13]

War pacifism is of course the paradigmatic (and most common) type of pacifism, because war in general is the central moral problem or issue with which pacifism tends to be concerned. The pledge of War Resisters' International, for example, states: 'War is a crime against humanity. We therefore are determined not to support any kind of war and to strive for the removal of all causes of war.'[14] Similarly, Peter Mayer refers to the popular or conventional understanding of pacifism as 'the absolute refusal to participate in, or support in any way, the waging of war'.[15] Thus, pacifism is conventionally defined as the principle that it is morally wrong to initiate or participate in war.

This of course begs the crucial question as to *why* it is wrong to participate in war, and the answer is sometimes provided in terms of the amount or type of either killing or violence involved in war. Richard Norman, for example, suggests that the more general moral principle that underlies the pacifist prohibition against participation in war or the use of armed force is the wrongness of killing human beings. 'Pacifism … is a principled position, and the relevant principle to which it appeals is the principle of not taking human life.'[16] In this case, of course, war pacifism becomes a variety of killing pacifism.

For some pacifists, however, the objection is to war as such, or the use of armed force as an instrument of either foreign policy or social change, rather than a more general condemnation of violence or killing under all circumstances. Thus, there are other moral reasons advanced in favour of antiwar pacifism, in addition to a general prohibition against the taking of human life. What Brock and Young refer to as the 'Utilitarian Approach', for example, refers to the 'enormous cost and wastefulness of modern war'.[17] The implication is that the resources expended on war and preparations for war could achieve far more to satisfy the basic needs or promote the wellbeing of humanity if used in some other way. More particularly, war is a struggle between powerful countries over economic interests that does little to benefit the mass of humankind. Furthermore, in an era of weapons of mass destruction, 'the realisation of the utilitarian principle of the greatest happiness of the greatest number' requires 'an unequivocal renunciation of war'.[18]

Similarly, war as a particular instrument of foreign policy is sometimes condemned as a violation of international law, or at least of international norms of conflict resolution and prevention. Thus, war is distinguished from the use of armed force in self-defence or as a means of law enforcement, which are conceded to be morally permissible. The UN Charter, with its two exceptions to a more general prohibition against the use of armed force to deal with international conflict (Articles 42 and 51), reflects this more limited attempt to eliminate war as such as a feature of international politics. Nigel Young, for example, includes as pacifism 'war resistance or conscientious objection which is usually confined to fighting in national wars and does not include taking human life in self-defense or in defense of an accepted system of international law – or for the internal maintenance of a democratically elected government'.[19]

Russell, writing during World War I, argued in favour of the effectiveness of 'passive resistance', or nonviolence, as the basis of national defence. He conceded, however, that the elimination of war as a feature of international politics was more likely to be achieved through establishing 'a central government of the world', capable of enforcing 'the reign of law'.[20] The use of force to implement the rule of law at this level would correspond to the role of a global police force rather than an army, however.[21]

In general, then, we can distinguish three components or varieties of antiwar pacifism or antimilitarism. The first of these we can call humanitarian (or deontological) pacifism. This involves opposition to war based on more general moral principles, such as a general prohibition against the taking of human life or the use of violence.

In some cases, such as the Quakers and the other historic peace churches, this prohibition is derived from specific religious beliefs. Such Christian pacifists, including Tolstoy, saw 'the Sermon on the Mount as central to their case against war'.[22] For Tolstoy, pacifism or nonresistance 'was a personal obligation from which there was no exemption', which furthermore 'formed the core of the Gospels'.[23] The Sermon on the Mount (as well as the Decalogue) 'forbade killing a being created in the image of God', thus reiterating 'the sanctity of human life'.[24]

A second source of antiwar pacifism is internationalism, which opposes war as a violation of international law, multilateralism and collective security. Brock and Young suggest that one of the weaknesses of a one-dimensional emphasis on international law and international institutions is that this overlooks issues of power, class and economics. In particular, it does not 'penetrate the relationship between war and the economic order nor ... detect the hidden seeds of war in the exploitation of labor'.[25]

This theme is the basis of a third source of antiwar pacifism, socialist or egalitarian antimilitarism, which challenges war as a vehicle for pursuing elite economic interests.

War, most socialists believed, resulted from the inevitable clash of economic rivalries ... And in wars the workers suffered, but not the capitalists that fomented them.[26]

This specifically class-based form of antiwar pacifism is sometimes connected to utilitarian antimilitarism, based on a critique of war as a wasteful or destructive use of scarce resources. Russell, for instance, utilised such arguments in his seminal essay 'The Ethics of War', written during the first year of World War I. He wrote that 'war, and the fear of war' retards social progress because 'it diminishes the resources available for improving the condition of the wage-earning classes'.[27]

This suspicion that war serves the private interests of the powerful few at the expense of the mass of humanity appears in many forms, however. During the sixteenth century, for example, we find Erasmus writing that 'the greatest share of the calamities inseparable from a state of war falls to those persons who have no interest, no concern whatever, either in the cause, or the success of the war'.[28] And furthermore: 'If you look narrowly into the case, you will find that they are, chiefly, the private, sinister, and selfish motives of princes, which operate as the real causes of all war'.[29] Similarly, both Rousseau and Kant argued that democracy, or at least a republican form of government, was the best cure for war, 'since wars were waged by princes in their own interest and not in that of their peoples'.[30]

During the interwar period of the last century, between World War I and World War II, as Brock and Young point out, these three varieties of antimilitarism were temporarily united in their opposition to war and preparations for war. Internationalists abandoned antimilitarism, however, after the accession of Hitler to power and the invasion of Abyssinia (Ethiopia) by Italy because of the threat these posed to the international community, the defence of which was their primary concern. Socialists, on the other hand, abandoned pacifism in response to the Spanish Civil War, because of the threat by Franco to a left-wing Republican government, and the threat of fascism to socialism more generally.[31]

## II. PACIFISM AND JUST WAR THEORY

A distinction is sometimes made between so-called 'absolute' pacifism and various forms of 'contingent' pacifism. According to Coates, for example:

> For one version of pacifism there are no conceivable circumstances in which war is morally permissible. The moral prohibition of war is an absolute one. Other forms of 'pacifism' are more selective, prohibiting war in some circumstances but not in others. This 'contingent' form of pacifism accepts the moral permissibility of war, at least in principle.[32]

Peter Mayer writes, for example, that the association of pacifism with 'the absolute refusal to participate in any war dates back to World War I', and was at least partly a response to national conscription. 'The term pacifism became firmly associated in the public mind with the absolute position, implying a personal refusal to fight.'[33] Internationalism, on the other hand, as embodied in the UN Charter, prohibits war as an instrument of foreign policy, but permits the use of armed force in self-defence or to enforce international law in the form of Security Council resolutions.

I would suggest, however, that this distinction between absolute and contingent forms of pacifism is somewhat artificial. As we have seen, the most interesting and the most influential forms of pacifism all depend on some process of moral reasoning to support their opposition to war, so in this sense all varieties of pacifism are contingent upon the credibility of the particular reasons they give for opposing war.

I think the crucial distinction is between pacifism and other forms of antimilitarism. Pacifism as such is primarily a moral position. For the genuine or fully fledged pacifist, then, ethical (and specifically deontological) considerations will ultimately supersede other considerations when making decisions about war and the use of armed force.

'Humanitarian pacifism' is genuinely pacifist in this sense, because its opposition to war is derived primarily from ethical concerns about killing or the use of violence. The socialist or egalitarian critique and internationalism, on the other hand, are primarily concerned about the economic, political or social implications or consequences of war. Cady agrees that: 'Varieties of pacifism toward the … weaker end of the scale are grounded in greater concern for anticipated results or effects of acts of war than on duties to which we are bound independently of consequences.'[34] Thus, while they remain forms of antimilitarism, they are not fully pacifist positions.

The opposition to war of humanitarian pacifism is much more stringent than that of other varieties of antimilitarism, precisely because it is based primarily on ethical considerations or principles. It is virtually impossible to imagine a war that did not involve some killing, for example, whereas, as we have seen, the use of armed force as a means of enforcing international law tends to be accepted by internationalist antimilitarists, even though they oppose war as an instrument of foreign policy.

It could be argued that the moral content of both the egalitarian or utilitarian approach and internationalism, as antiwar positions, can be interpreted in terms of just war theory, and *jus ad bellum* criteria in particular. Utilitarian antimilitarism is concerned about issues of proportionality, given the tremendous cost and destructiveness associated with war and preparations for war. Erasmus argued against war, more on humanist grounds, 'that no war whatever did, at any time, succeed so fortunately as not to produce more loss than gain, more evil than good'.[35] Internationalism, on the other hand, is connected to the issue of just cause, with immediate self-defence as the only circumstance under which the unilateral use of armed force is permitted by the UN Charter.

Humanitarian pacifism, however, is a distinctive moral position precisely because it depends on a stronger moral principle than its equivalent in just war theory. Thus, the humanitarian pacifist prohibition against state-sponsored killing under any circumstance is much stronger than the *jus in bello* criterion of discrimination, which prohibits the deliberate killing of noncombatants but permits the killing of combatants as well as the unintended killing of noncombatants (in accordance with the principle of double effect). Richard Norman, for example, writes that noncombatant immunity constitutes 'an important point of disagreement' between just war theory and pacifism because 'the "just war" theorist says about the killing of noncombatants what the pacifist says about all killing in war: that it must not be done, even as a means of resistance against aggression'.[36] This is another reason for identifying the humanitarian or deontological position as uniquely pacifist, as distinct from internationalist or egalitarian antimilitarism.

## III. PACIFISM AND POLITICAL THEORY

Humanitarian pacifism is primarily a moral position, involving the personal refusal to participate in war for ethical reasons. As such, it does not provide or possess a political theory, or a theory of international relations, which might both explain why wars occur as well as how the international system might be structured differently so as to avoid or eliminate them. This reflects a tension perhaps between the political requirements of internationalist and egalitarian antimilitarism on the one hand, and the ethical requirements of humanitarian pacifism on the other.

Instead, as a moral position, pacifism is often presented in individualistic or sectarian terms. In other words, the refusal to participate in war is often presented as a matter for an individual's conscience, sometimes justified by their membership in a particular religious (or political) sect or group. Mayer refers to such pacifism as relying 'on a personal testimony against violence – individual *acts* of conscience'.[37] It is for this reason that pacifism is often associated with conscientious objection to military service on the part of individuals or members of specific groups.

The main problem with such individual or sectarian pacifism is that it can coexist with the continued use of war and armed conflict, providing those individuals or groups who so desire are not required or compelled to participate. According to John Rawls, such vocational pacifism 'no more challenges the state's authority [to engage in war] than the celibacy of priests challenges the sanctity of marriage'.[38]

Pacifism as a matter for individual choice or conscience can coexist with war as a social and political institution. It becomes an option for some but not an obligation for all. It seems more concerned with the expression of individual or group dissent, than with promoting political and social change to minimise or even eliminate war and armed conflict. Thus, Brock and Young refer to Ceadel's suggestion that 'for most pacifists social service was a means of atoning for being a tolerated sect without a political solution to offer'.[39]

They also suggest that while nonviolent political action has demonstrated its effectiveness in dealing with internal or domestic oppression, it has yet to do so as a response to war or armed conflict.[40] In the case of Gandhi in India, for example:

> The techniques of *satyagraha* were applied by the Mahatma exclusively to group relations within the state. International relations were a branch of politics on which Indians under British rule could make little impact.[41]

Although Gandhi 'insisted ... on the relevance of nonviolence as an instrument for obtaining and maintaining peace and justice in the relations between states',[42] the task for pacifism nonetheless is to find an equivalent to *satyagraha* as an effective political response to war and armed conflict. While there are some who suggest, based on historical experience, that 'organized, disciplined, mass-based, nonviolent direct action had successfully resisted foreign aggression and promoted social revolution under both liberal and authoritarian conditions',[43] there are others such as Coates who argue that 'the alternative defence strategies of non-violent resistance appear largely unconvincing'.[44]

As we shall see, however, this raises further questions concerning pacifism as a political theory. We need to ask whether or not pacifists should aim to provide alternative mechanisms for protecting conventional political structures, such as the nation-state, or whether they should aim at transforming such structures, precisely because they require and justify the use of armed force as their ultimate defence.

If it is to become more than the expression of individual or group dissent, pacifism requires a political theory or a theory of international relations that both explains and promotes its vision of a world without war. Ironically, as Coates has pointed out, pacifism's analysis of the morality of war coincides in some respects to a 'realist' interpretation of international politics:

> Pacifism in its pure or 'absolute' form shares with realism a deep moral scepticism about war. Both deny that war can ever be subject to moral limitation.[45]

The pacifist, however, views war as deeply immoral, whereas the realist regards it instead as merely amoral, or outside the boundaries of morality, which helps explain their differing responses to it. For the realist, war is an unavoidable feature of international politics, which must be used effectively in pursuit of the national interest. For the pacifist, on the other hand: 'War cannot be anything other than a moral obscenity, to which avoidance is the only proper response.'[46]

Another crucial difference between pacifism and realism, despite a shared moral scepticism about war, concerns the so-called 'double morality' of the private and the public realm, or the personal and the political. This position is associated with Reinhold Niebuhr as one of the original theologians of the realist approach to international politics. According to Neibuhr, 'human collectives are less moral than the individuals which compose them'.[47] The implication is that standards of morality that may apply at the level of relations between individuals cannot apply at the level of international relations. This would include, for example, the prohibition against killing.

Proponents of just war theory also operate within the framework of this double morality. 'St Augustine, for example, is thought to have understood Christ's message of non-resistance as a counsel of perfection applicable to the individual in his personal life but not to the soldier while acting in his public capacity as defender of the state or political community.' Private or personal nonviolence can be reconciled with the political use of armed force in accordance with just war principles.[48]

As Martin Wight points out, however, a distinguishing characteristic of pacifism is precisely that it does not accept this double morality. For pacifists, he writes, 'there is not a double standard of morality but a single one, and political ethics ought to be assimilated to private ethics'.[49] The prohibition against killing that applies to individuals also applies to states, and to those acting on behalf of states. The essence of pacifism remains the renunciation of war by individuals, derived ultimately from a personal moral commitment involving the translation of personal moral decisions into the wider political sphere.[50]

Furthermore, as Coates points out, pacifists suspect that an artificial distinction between public and private morality cannot be sustained in the context of war, largely to the detriment of private morality. Instead, the demands of war undermine the requirements of ordinary morality because, in their new role as 'soldier', individuals are expected to behave outside the boundaries of conventional ethics. This provides another source of pacifist opposition to war, through insisting that the requirements of private morality must be upheld under all circumstances, if they are not to be eroded completely.

## IV. REFORMIST VERSUS REVOLUTIONARY PACIFISM

Not only does pacifism require the assimilation of public or political ethics to private ethics, it also presents a challenge to conventional Western political theory, particularly as it concerns the central role of the state. For those pacifists who object to the use of violence under any circumstances, and not merely in the context of war, the role of the state presents a particular problem. In Western political theory, one of the defining features of the state is that it possesses a monopoly over the legitimate use of violence, both internally and externally. For such pacifists, however, there can never be a legitimate use of violence, and this undermines a central function of the state. As Coates suggests:

> Some form of anarchism would appear to be the logical conclusion of so universal a form of pacifism, since from this radical perspective the state constitutes a form of institutionalised violence and a source of moral corruption.[51]

Such pacifism objects to a form of political and social organisation that depends on the use of violence as its ultimate sanction. Martin Wight also equates anarchism as a political theory with pacifism in international theory [sic].[52]

Thus, Brock and Young refer to Tolstoy as a 'Christian anarchist'. 'The state, in his view, must be dismantled entirely and replaced by a voluntarist society before nonviolence could be fully effective.'[53] They go on to suggest 'democratic decentralization ... has been the most usual political expression of twentieth-century pacifism'.[54]

Brock argues that Tolstoy is responsible for reviving and expanding the appeal of pacifism in the twentieth century for two reasons. First, he 'asserted the universality of pacifism and nonviolence as a rule of ethics',[55] so that it was no longer merely a matter of individual or small group conscience. Secondly, he accepted the political implications of this universal pacifist ethic through his arguments for wider social change. In an important sense, Gandhi is the intellectual (and practical) heir of Tolstoy because he also combined the pacifist or nonviolent moral impulse (*ahimsa*) with efforts to achieve fundamental political and social change through mass nonviolent civil resistance (*satyagraha*).[56]

Pacifists sometimes combined an anarchist critique of the state, however nascent, with a socialist critique of capitalism. They felt they must 'work for a classless society in which cooperation replaces competition as the goal of human actions', because such economic competition can result ultimately in war. Furthermore: 'Without tackling the roots of war in a faulty economic system, moral protest remained an empty gesture.'[57]

The distinction between this position and the socialist antimilitarism outlined earlier is that it retains the moral objection to the killing of human beings in the context of the wars that result inevitably from capitalism as its central concern. Socialist antimilitarism, on the other hand, objects to war as a means of re-enforcing and exacerbating existing global inequalities and injustices.

In their comprehensive history of pacifism in the twentieth century, Brock and Young claim that in Britain and the US:

> The pacifist movement ... tended to regard a society which retained a vital local democracy alongside a developed system of communal welfare as the best guarantee for a peaceable world. On the European continent pacifists were often drawn from circles influenced by the libertarian anarcho-syndicalist tradition.[58]

Both approaches shared a suspicion of a strong centralised state and a commitment to cooperation rather than competition as the basis for an economy that served human needs rather than private profit. Tolstoy went so far as to question 'the institution of property' itself, again in the anarchist tradition, 'at least insofar as property required force to defend it'.[59] He also suggested 'armies are only needed by governments in order to dominate their own working-classes'. 'Defence against foreign enemies is only an excuse.'[60]

The importance of this implicit anarcho-socialism is that it suggests domestic social and political revolution is a necessary precursor to the elimination of war and armed conflict and the transformation of international politics. In a sense, domestic social and political change provides the necessary link between pacifism as an individual and personal ethic and the elimination of war as a feature of international relations. Again, according to Brock, Tolstoy made this connection explicit: 'Tolstoy introduced a new note into the pacifist argument when he pleaded for a radical, if somewhat vague, restructuring of society as an essential prerequisite for establishing international peace and brotherhood.'[61] The political organisation of society, and patterns of ownership of economic resources and the means of production, must be radically altered for pacifism to become effective and relevant in the international realm as well as a distinctive moral position.

This points to a crucial distinction, to which I alluded earlier, between reformist and revolutionary versions of pacifism. Reformist pacifism seeks alternative, nonviolent methods for defending conventional political structures, such as the nation-state. These most often take the form of various proposals for 'civilian-based defence', for example. Revolutionary pacifism, on the other hand, requires a transformation of conventional economic and political structures as a means of eliminating war and armed conflict as features of international relations.

## V. PACIFISM AND COSMOPOLITANISM

It is this latter form of revolutionary pacifism that connects most obviously to cosmopolitanism as a theory of international relations, precisely because it argues that we must transcend or replace the nation-state as the central institution of both domestic and international politics. The cosmopolitan commitment to a more polycentric political order is reflected in recent discussions about 'cosmopolitan democracy' and 'global citizenship', for example.[62] The functional or instrumental value of the state is to be emphasised, along with that of other levels of political community, as distinct from its priority as the primary unit of political affairs, whether domestic or international.

As discussed in Chapter 4, some authors (such as Mary Kaldor) emphasise the significance of civil society, both locally and globally, as part of this polycentric political order.[63] Civil society represents the space between the individual (as citizen) and the state (as sovereign political entity) available for autonomous political and social organisations. It provides a normative and institutional basis for cosmopolitanism that is distinct from the state and conventional state sovereignty.

Thus, cosmopolitanism rests on a kind of ontological individualism, according to which individual human beings (rather than, for example, states) are the basic constituents of political community, whether local, national, international or global. The Westphalian state, although it currently dominates the international system, is a product of history and of human agency in the same way that other forms of political organisation have been. The state, as both idea and institution, is historically, politically, ethically and ontologically contingent in a way that human beings are not.

This ontological individualism provides the moral impetus behind the cosmopolitan respect for human beings over and above particular political institutions or forms of social organisation. Similarly, in ethical terms, humanitarian or deontological pacifism is derived ultimately from a fundamental respect for the value of every human life, whatever their politically defined role or status.

In other words, it can be argued that pacifism and cosmopolitanism converge in both their ethical and political dimensions. This convergence is reflected in Bertrand Russell's claim, during World War I, that 'war will only end after a great labour has been performed in altering men's [sic] moral ideals, directing them to the good of mankind, and not only of the separate nations into which men happen to have been born'.[64]

At the ethical level, humanitarian pacifism and cosmopolitanism share a commitment to the equal value of each human being as a member of a universal moral community. At the political level, both revolutionary pacifism and cosmopolitanism query state sovereignty as the primary value or principle of political community and the nation-state as the central institution of both domestic and international politics. It is in this sense that cosmopolitanism can provide a more general political theory encompassing revolutionary, humanitarian pacifism.

# NOTES

1. Coates, *The Ethics of War*, p. 77.
2. Wight, *International Theory*, pp. 108–9.
3. Brock and Young, *Pacifism in the Twentieth Century*, p. 6.
4. Ibid. p. 12.
5. Ceadel, *Thinking about Peace and War*, pp. 141–5.
6. Ibid. p. 143.
7. Russell, 'Inconsistency?', p. 323.
8. Russell, 'The Ethics of War', p. 127.
9. Russell, 'Inconsistency?', p. 323.
10. Cady, *From Warism to Pacifism*, p. 66.
11. Ibid. pp. 69–70.
12. Coates, *The Ethics of War*, pp. 80–1.
13. Russell, 'Man's Peril', p. 320.
14. Cited in Brock and Young, *Pacifism in the Twentieth Century*, p. 103.
15. Mayer, 'Introduction', p. 11.
16. Norman, 'The Case for Pacifism', p. 166.
17. Brock and Young, *Pacifism in the Twentieth Century*, p. 107.
18. Ibid. p. 109.
19. Young, 'Preface', p. x.
20. Russell, 'War and Non-Resistance', p.56.
21. Ibid. pp. 39–40.
22. Brock, *Varieties of Pacifism*, p. 48.
23. Ibid. p. 85.
24. Ibid. p. 87.
25. Brock and Young, *Pacifism in the Twentieth Century*, p. 13.
26. Ibid. p. 14.
27. Russell, 'The Ethics of War', p. 132.
28. Erasmus, 'Letter to Anthony a Bergis', p. 56.
29. Ibid. p. 59.
30. Carr, *The Twenty Years' Crisis 1919–1939*, p. 25.
31. Brock and Young, *Pacifism in the Twentieth Century*, p. 121, and Chapter IV more generally.
32. Coates, *The Ethics of War*, pp. 78–9.
33. Mayer, 'Introduction', p. 23.
34. Cady, *From Warism to Pacifism*, pp. 65–6.
35. Erasmus, 'Letter to Anthony a Bergis', p. 56.
36. Norman, 'The Case for Pacifism', p. 174.
37. Mayer, 'Introduction', p. 22.
38. Rawls, *A Theory of Justice*, p. 382.

39. Brock and Young, *Pacifism in the Twentieth Century*, p. 168.
40. Ibid. p. 262.
41. Ibid. p. 81.
42. Ibid. p. 81.
43. Bennett, 'Socialist Pacifism and Nonviolent Social Revolution', p. 105.
44. Coates, *The Ethics of War*, p. 115.
45. Ibid. p. 82.
46. Ibid. p. 82.
47. As paraphrased in Macgregor, 'The relevance of an impossible ideal', p. 19. Niebuhr develops this theme in his book *Moral Man and Immoral Society*.
48. Coates, *The Ethics of War*, p. 78.
49. Wight, *International Theory*, p. 255.
50. Cf. Brock, *Varieties of Pacifism*, p. 90.
51. Coates, *The Ethics of War*, pp. 86–7.
52. Wight, *International Theory*, p. 108.
53. Brock and Young, *Pacifism in the Twentieth Century*, p. 6.
54. Ibid. p. 37.
55. Brock, *Varieties of Pacifism*, p. 90.
56. Ibid. p. 90.
57. Brock and Young, *Pacifism in the Twentieth Century*, p. 113.
58. Ibid. pp. 113–14.
59. Brock, *Varieties of Pacifism*, p. 85.
60. Tolstoy, 'Letter to a Non-commissioned Officer', p. 161.
61. Brock, *Varieties of Pacifism*, p. 90.
62. See, for example, Archibugi, Held and Köhler, *Re-imagining Political Community* and Dower and Williams, *Global Citizenship*.
63. See, for example, Kaldor, *New and Old Wars*.
64. Russell, 'War and Non-Resistance', p. 57.

# PART III
## COSMOPOLITAN STRATEGIES

# CHAPTER 7

# POST-MODERN WAR

'State failure' conflicts in the 1990s suggested that war was perhaps entering a new, 'post-modern' phase in which the state could no longer claim a central role in either controlling or utilising organised political violence. This changing nature of armed conflict was illustrated most dramatically by the Al Qaeda attacks on the World Trade Center and the Pentagon in September 2001. The subsequent US war on Iraq, on the other hand, represents the projection of state power to achieve foreign policy objectives in a much more conventional way. The combined implications of state failure and US hegemony in the post-Cold War international situation suggest state-building, global governance and transnational civil society as complementary responses to the challenges of armed conflict and political violence in the new millennium. On the other hand, cosmopolitanism may require responses to war and armed conflict that do not depend on conventional state-based conceptions of security.

## I. CONTEMPORARY ARMED CONFLICT

Many contemporary armed conflicts seem to share certain characteristics that differentiate them from conventional war as a discrete phenomenon involving the large-scale use of organised military force between states over resources and territory or other easily identifiable strategic and political objectives. The key characteristics of these armed conflicts are:

1. they are often internal or 'intra-state' rather than between states or countries;
2. they involve the 'privatisation' of war, that is, nonstate actors play a prominent role;
3. they involve the 'civilianisation' of casualties; and
4. they endure over protracted periods of time.

Others have described these wars as 'post-modern conflicts' or 'forgotten wars', and in the development literature they have been referred to as 'complex political emergencies'.

Concerning the first of these characteristics, it has been suggested: 'Most contemporary war is civil war and almost all of it occurs in poor countries.'[1] Of the 96 armed conflicts between 1989 and 1995, for example, only five were between states; the other 91 were intra-state.

Project Ploughshares, a Canadian inter-church nongovernmental organisation, has distinguished usefully between 'three overlapping types of intrastate war: state control, state formation, and state failure'. State control conflicts 'centre on struggles for control of the governing apparatus of the state', and can be motivated by political ideology, 'communal and ethnic interests' or religion.[2]

State formation conflicts 'centre on the form or shape of the state itself and generally involve particular regions of a country fighting for a greater measure of autonomy or for outright secession'. Such conflicts are often identity-based (ethnicity and religion, for example), and include the wars in Sri Lanka and in former Yugoslavia in the 1990s.[3]

Finally, there are 'failed state wars … in which the armed conflict is … about local issues and disputes involving violence in the absence of effective government control'. Conflict in Somalia continues to be 'an obvious example of a generalized chaos that grew out of the failure of all state authority, which in turn was the product of a state control war to overthrow a corrupt regime'. Furthermore, such conflicts are not exclusive and some countries (such as Sudan) 'have the misfortune of hosting all three types of war'.[4]

A second, and related, feature of contemporary armed conflict is the so-called 'privatisation' of war through the extensive involvement of nonstate actors. Internal wars often involve conflict between government forces and nonstate actors such as armed opposition groups, militias and armed gangs of various types because 'internal conflicts typically pit a state against part or parts of its society'.[5] Furthermore, some armed conflicts, such as those characterised by failed states, may only involve such nonstate actors, between various paramilitary groups for example.

Andrew Latham points out that this occurs in the context of much wider processes of privatisation, producing 'a decidedly *postmodern* form of the state – sometimes called the "neoliberal state" – that has transferred to private authorities many of the powers and responsibilities it had previously reserved to itself', particularly in the economic and social spheres.[6] Similarly, M. L. R. Smith refers to 'the capacity of economic globalisation to erode state authority and stimulate internal substate challenges resulting in violent disintegration'.[7]

A third characteristic of contemporary armed conflict is the 'civilian-isation' of casualties, through the deliberate targeting of civilians. 'The striking feature of contemporary warfare is the use of noncombatants as instruments and objectives of warfare.'[8] Such wars often involve violence, in the form of gross human rights violations, being perpetrated by both government forces and armed opposition groups against the civilian population of the country. Governments, for example, use violence not merely to deal with armed opposition groups, but to crush any form of dissent or resistance. This is connected to the internal or intra-state nature of armed conflict, because, it has been suggested, most armies are used for domestic containment rather than external war.

Furthermore, not only is political violence directed against unarmed political opponents, it can also be directed deliberately against civilian populations in general, without much if any political involvement. In such internal wars, government forces and armed opposition groups often spend less time and fewer resources fighting each other than targeting unarmed civilians, because they both view whole sections of the population as the enemy. The extensive use of 'ethnic cleansing', or genocide, in the Balkans, Rwanda and East Timor is an example of this.

In the context of contemporary armed conflict, the moral and legal principle of noncombatant immunity is not merely eroded, it is deliber-ately violated, as Kaldor points out.

> Because destabilization and population displacement are the goals rather than the destruction of a clearly defined opponent, what used to be side-effects have now become central to the fighting. Conspicuous atrocity, systematic rape, hostage-taking, forced starvation and siege, destruction of religious and historic monu-ments, the use of shells and rockets against civilian targets (especially homes, hospitals or crowded places like markets or water sources), the use of land mines to make large areas uninhabitable, are all deliberate components of military strategy.[9]

Civilians or noncombatants are injured, killed and abused not merely incidentally but quite deliberately by the protagonists in such wars.

The privatisation of the use of armed force and the dissipation of political control over those who employ it may also contribute to the civilianisation of casualties. Armed conflicts 'are frequently fought by militia forces and other armed groups, with little sense of discipline, a poorly defined chain of command and no discernible political pro-gramme'.[10] In the absence of such structures and objectives, it is difficult for an armed group 'to establish rules of conduct towards civilian popula-tions and to develop enforcement mechanisms to this effect'.[11]

This may at least partly account for the rising toll of civilian casualties in contemporary warfare. It has been suggested that 95 per cent of the casualties of internal wars are civilians; that is, that civilians are the deliberate targets of domestic military violence.

A final characteristic of contemporary armed conflicts is their lengthy duration, since they often arise from or are expressions of so-called 'protracted social conflicts'. Many of these armed conflicts have lasted for decades, if not generations (for example, Angola, Sri Lanka, Colombia). The end of the Cold War, however, has made their distinguishing characteristics more obvious or prominent.

Although each armed conflict must be treated as unique, in terms of its causes, dynamics and possible resolution, we can perhaps identify some common sources or origins. These suggestions are by no means exhaustive, nor are they exclusive, in the sense that each suggested cause may contribute to any given armed conflict.

Thus, the origins of contemporary armed conflict can be analysed in terms of:

1. 'political economy', that is, so-called 'resource-based' conflicts;
2. 'political culture', that is, 'identity-based' conflicts;
3. outside intervention or interference; and
4. 'structural violence', that is, poverty and inequality.

Examples of resource-based conflicts include Sierra Leone (diamonds), Sudan (oil), Angola (diamonds and oil) and Cambodia (tropical timber and drugs). Armed conflict can be fought in order to achieve control over such natural resources. Furthermore, access to or control over political power can be a source of competition or conflict within a country or a society, where such power can be seen as a 'resource' to be fought over.

The economies of many developing countries, for example, are hugely dependent on development assistance from so-called developed countries. This 'official development assistance' (ODA) is provided to the governments of developing countries in the form of either bilateral or multilateral aid, so that 'access to the administration of development aid was based on one's ability to control the state'.[12] The same applies to the large sums of military aid provided from arms-exporting to arms-importing countries. In other words, the state, as recipient of these forms of economic assistance, becomes a resource to be fought over.

However, armed conflict as such can also generate economic benefits for the various armed groups involved in the form of weapons sales, protection rackets and so on, so that once the fighting stops these material benefits disappear. These benefits can produce self-perpetuating or 'predatory' armed conflicts. In the context of the civil war in Sudan between the government and rebel forces in the south of the country, which began in 1983, David Keen writes:

'Winning the war' was not the sole, or even the most important, objective of many
of those engaging in violence. The primary goal for many was to manipulate
violence in ways that achieved economic goals.[13]

Keen refers to the role of army officers in restricting grain movements to
southern Sudan in order to shape grain markets in cooperation with
merchants, 'to their mutual advantage'.[14] Bringing an end to the conflict
would remove the opportunity for armed groups to engage in such
predatory behaviour.

Identity-based conflicts include conflicts where religion and ethnicity
play a role, such as in Sri Lanka. The origins of many armed conflicts 'lie
in relations between enduring identity groups, which do not necessarily
correspond with existing nation-state boundaries'. Thus, many contemporary internal conflicts are characterised as 'a prolonged and often violent
struggle by communal groups for such basic needs as security, recognition and acceptance, fair access to political institutions and economic
participation'.[15] As we shall see, the civil war in Sri Lanka demonstrates
that if you deny minority groups access to political power, they can
eventually feel they have no choice but to resort to armed struggle.

Foreign intervention or involvement can add a crucial dimension to
armed conflict, even where it occurs primarily within states or countries.
According to Harris and Lewis, for example: 'Some internal conflicts,
such as those in Angola, Afghanistan and El Salvador, have been as much
external as domestic in nature, with the intensity, scope and duration of
these conflicts affected by the interaction between domestic events and
external responses.'[16] This can also be said about the civil war in Mozambique between Frelimo and Renamo (discussed in Chapter 10), which
was at its height during the Cold War, as well as the ongoing conflict in
Sri Lanka.

Structural violence refers to the political, economic and social structures that maintain gross disparities of wealth and power within a country,
such as so-called 'economic apartheid' in South Africa and Brazil (based
on highly unequal patterns of land ownership, for example). Furthermore,
there are intimate links between structural violence and direct violence,
because direct or physical violence is often used against those who try to
resist or overcome structural violence.

## II. SRI LANKA AS A 'STATE FORMATION' CONFLICT

Sri Lanka provides an example of a protracted internal armed conflict
where tentative steps towards some sort of peaceful resolution have been
made over the last few years. Sri Lanka is an island, roughly the size of

Ireland, in the Indian Ocean near the Indian state of Tamil Nadu. It has a population of approximately 20 million, which makes it more densely populated than India.

There are four main 'ethnic groups' in Sri Lanka. The Sinhalese form 74 per cent of the population, Ceylon Tamils 13 per cent, Muslims 7 per cent, and Up-Country Tamils 6 per cent. The Sinhalese are mostly Buddhist, the Tamils mostly Hindu, with a small number of Christians from both communities. Sinhala and Tamil are the two main indigenous languages, with English as the main colonial language. The Muslims are Tamil-speaking.

The Sinhalese are the majority in the south and west of Sri Lanka. The Ceylon Tamils are a majority in the north of the country. The Muslims are concentrated in the east, and the Up-Country Tamils in the centre. The Up-Country Tamils were brought over as indentured labourers by the British to work on their coffee plantations, which subsequently became Sri Lanka's famous tea plantations.

The Liberation Tigers of Tamil Eelam (LTTE) have been fighting for an independent homeland, Tamil Eelam, in the north and east of the country since the 1970s. The conflict to date has cost the lives of tens of thousands of soldiers and civilians, and displaced up to a million people. Both government forces and the LTTE have deliberately targeted civilian populations as part of their struggle for political supremacy in disputed areas. The LTTE, for example, have used armed attacks against Muslims in an attempt to force them from the north and east of the country.[17]

Factors contributing to the conflict in Sri Lanka include: (1) constitutional failure, (2) the 'double minority' complex, and (3) the role of India as the regional power. The issue of constitutional failure helps define the conflict in Sri Lanka as an example of a 'state formation' conflict, concerning territorial boundaries in a post-colonial state. Sri Lanka, or Ceylon as it was known then, acquired political independence from British colonial rule in 1948. The civil war in Sri Lanka reflects the failure of both Sinhalese and Tamil ruling elites 'to find an acceptable constitutional arrangement to manage the affairs of a pluralistic society'.[18] The role of the sangha, the hierarchy of Sri Lanka's Buddhist monks, has been crucial in promoting a particularly virulent and aggressive form of Sinhalese nationalism.

The imposition of the 'Sinhala Only' Act in 1956 (modified in 1987 following the Indo-Lanka Accord) illustrates the dangers of majoritarian democracy in a unitary state in Sri Lanka (then Ceylon), given its ethnic composition. Sinhala became the sole official language of the country, negatively affecting Tamil access to government services and public sector employment. 'The passing of the Official Language Act of July 1956 –

which is often referred to as "Sinhala Only" – was a major step towards defining Ceylon as a primarily Sinhala state.'[19]

The new constitution of 1972, which 'made Ceylon a republic, henceforth called Sri Lanka', entrenched these provisions even further. 'The new constitution guaranteed the supreme position in Sri Lanka of the Sinhala language and of Buddhism, at the expense of Tamil and of other religions.'[20]

Similarly, in August 1983 (following the anti-Tamil riots the previous month), the government introduced 'a constitutional amendment banning advocacy of secessionism, even by peaceful, political means'.[21] All political parties advocating separatism were proscribed and it became compulsory for members of parliament to take an oath rejecting separatism.[22] As a result, members of the Tamil political party (the Tamil United Liberation Front, or TULF) had to forfeit their seats in parliament, because they had been elected on a separatist platform, removing the possibility of parliamentary dialogue and handing the initiative over to young Tamil militants committed to armed struggle. 'The constitutional path for Tamil nationalist aspirations was effectively blocked.'[23] It is important to note that the political violence employed by the LTTE followed prolonged efforts by various Tamil groups to pursue their political objectives peacefully and constitutionally, going back to the negotiations preceding political independence in 1948.[24]

What is required is a constitution that facilitates inclusive rather than majoritarian democracy, according to Radhika Coomaraswamy, Sri Lankan Tamil and United Nations Human Rights Commission's rapporteur on violence against women. The basis of any such reforms 'should be the recognition that Sri Lankan society is plural in its ethnic composition'[25] and that political structures must reflect this.

The civil war in Sri Lanka also reflects a so-called 'double minority' complex on the part of the two main ethnic groups, demonstrating the salience of identity as a cause of the conflict. The Tamils are a minority within Sri Lanka, but 'the Sinhalese too feel themselves to be a minority community considering that 60 million Tamils live in Tamil Nadu', the south Indian state closest to Sri Lanka.[26]

Thus, Sinhalese political leaders rejected a federal as opposed to a unitary constitution because they feared a separate or autonomous Tamil state in the north-east of the country would be dominated by India. Tamils, on the other hand, felt threatened demographically and territorially by the central government's agricultural policy, which involved transferring Sinhalese into the less densely populated north-east of the country.

Finally, India has often played a destabilising role in the conflict through its support for Tamil militants, and the LTTE in particular, especially in its early phases. In the 1980s, for example, more than 20,000 militants were based in India, being trained by RAW, the Research and Analysis Wing, the foreign intelligence agency of the Indian government.[27]

The height of India's involvement occurred during the late 1980s, following the so-called Indo-Lanka Accord between the two governments in 1987. Under the terms of the accord, tens of thousands of Indian troops, in the form of the so-called Indian Peace-Keeping Force (or IPKF) entered the north-east of the country in an attempt to disarm the LTTE.[28]

As Peter Kloos points out: 'The arrival of the IPKF, however, had an unanticipated effect: it estranged the Sinhala political elite from the Sinhala masses' resulting in 'an almost complete breakdown of Sri Lankan society'. The Sri Lankan government had to deal simultaneously with the LTTE and the presence of the IPKF in the north of the country and an insurrection led by the radical nationalist Sinhalese JVP (Janatha Vimukthi Peramuna) in the south.

> Official and unofficial government violence, LTTE and JVP violence, and violence perpetrated to settle private quarrels or for material gain became indistinguishable: it was no longer quite clear who killed who and for what reason. Due to methods of killing and the tyre-burning of victims it was often not even clear who had been killed. Tens of thousands just disappeared, leaving no trace (the number of disappearances is estimated at 40–60,000 …) This period is referred to by Sinhala as the *beeshanaya kale*, the time of terror.[29]

The confluence of a 'state formation' conflict in the north and east of the country and a 'state control' insurrection in the south very nearly resulted in the overthrow of the central government and the disintegration of the Sri Lankan political system, or 'state failure'.

The ruthless suppression of the JVP, including the extra-judicial execution of its leadership, in late 1989, followed by the departure of Indian troops by March 1990 brought an end to the political crisis, at least temporarily, however. Indian involvement has been less overt since the LTTE assassinated Indian Prime Minister Rajiv Gandhi during the Indian election campaign of 1991.

The latest and most promising round of peace talks to end the conflict began in September 2002, following the election of a new government in December 2001 and a ceasefire negotiated by Norway in February 2002. During the 2001 elections Tamils 'in the north and east mostly voted for the Tamil National Alliance (TNA), comprising four political parties that supported direct talks between the government and the LTTE and recognition of the LTTE as the sole Tamil representative at these talks'.[30] In other words, the election result provided legitimacy to the LTTE's role within the peace talks.

During the first round of talks in September 2002, the LTTE made a crucial concession when they replaced their demand for full independence with an acceptance of autonomy. Their chief negotiator, Anton Balasingham, said: 'We demand the recognition of our homeland.' He also said, however: 'When we say homeland it doesn't mean separate state.'

Two factors may have influenced the LTTE's decision to enter into serious negotiations with the Sri Lankan government, one external and one internal.

The external factor may be the changed international climate concerning 'terrorist' organisations, especially since 11 September 2001. In the past decade, the LTTE has been declared a terrorist organisation by India, the United States, Britain, Canada and Australia. This has affected the Tigers' ability to raise funds internationally, especially from the Tamil diaspora. The significance of the LTTE's global reach to their success as a secessionist movement inside Sri Lanka cannot be overestimated. Kloos, for example, refers to them as 'a transnational enterprise, tapping financial and other sources wherever there are Tamils'.[31]

The US in particular has recently shown high-level interest in the conflict for perhaps the first time. In 2002, for example, Richard Armitage, US Deputy Secretary of State, visited Colombo and reiterated the US administration's support for the peace process. This is especially noteworthy given the traditional hostility of India, as the regional power, to any form of US presence in the region.

The internal factor may be the realisation by both the government and the LTTE that neither of them is going to win a military victory ('the hurting stalemate'), combined with a willingness to revise their original political or strategic objectives. This was facilitated initially by the elections of December 2001. 'The government and the LTTE realise that they cannot advance or achieve their respective political goals through military means and that their constituencies strongly desire a return to peace and stability.'[32] Furthermore, it is estimated that the 'war has cost the government up to one billion dollars a year in defence spending'. In 2001 'the country's GDP declined by 1.4 percent. Western diplomats believe this was partly responsible for pushing the government towards peace.'[33]

Thus, the protracted civil war in Sri Lanka exhibits many of the characteristics of contemporary armed conflict. It is a post-colonial state formation conflict, which has also triggered a state control war in the form of the JVP insurrection that almost resulted in state failure. All sides in these conflicts have deliberately targeted civilians, including the LTTE, the JVP and official and unofficial government forces, resulting in tens of thousands of deaths and disappearances. The success of the LTTE as a 'transnational enterprise' is an example of the 'privatisation' of armed conflict through nonstate actors.

## III. 'POST-MODERN' WAR AND STATE FAILURE

In the post-Cold War era, Mary Kaldor (and others) have referred to many armed conflicts as 'new wars' because they represent a departure from more conventional uses of organised political violence.[34] Such 'new' wars have also been described as 'post-modern' conflicts because they are characterised by the marginalisation of the state and its diminished capacity to control the use of armed force or violence in the territory under its jurisdiction.

Thus, post-modern war is a specific type or example of contemporary armed conflict, sharing but also heightening or exaggerating many of its distinguishing features, such as the centrality of nonstate actors and the deliberate targeting of a civilian population. Also, certain sources of contemporary armed conflict contribute to such post-modern wars, particularly identity politics and predatory economics, precisely because such activities undermine or challenge the significance of the state as a fundamental political entity.

Andrew Latham speaks 'of the history of warfare over the last millennium in terms of three broad epochs or eras': feudal, modern and post-modern war.[35] During the era of feudal war, 'the locus of control of the means of violence was dispersed across a diffuse community of arms-bearing fief-holders'.[36] Modern war, on the other hand, is characterised by the sovereign state's monopoly (or at least attempted monopoly) over organised violence. In other words, the sovereign state is the political entity 'exclusively qualified to impose peace internally and conduct war externally'.[37]

War became solely the prerogative of the state, so that 'by the high modern era, private wars were no longer tolerated, and the right to conduct war had become the exclusive right of the sovereign state'.[38] Latham concludes by suggesting that the transition from one era of warfare to the next (from feudal to modern to post-modern) is characterised by 'constitutive war', or 'a period in which wars are fought to determine the very ontology of the units entitled and able to exercise control over the means of violence'.[39]

As is suggested by the tripartite classification of internal or intra-state wars, the role of the state is central to our understanding of different types of contemporary armed conflict. Hedley Bull, for example, differentiated between 'loose' and 'strict' definitions of war based on the involvement of states. 'We should distinguish between war in the loose sense of organised violence which may be carried out by any political unit ... and war in the strict sense of international or interstate war, organised violence waged by sovereign states.'[40]

As we have seen, most examples of contemporary armed conflict conform more closely to Bull's 'loose' definition of war. According to Kaldor, for example, war can be defined as 'a conflict between politically-organized groups involving large-scale violence. This definition excludes acts of violence in which only one side is socially organized, for example, government repression or organized crime.'[41] The most distinctive characteristic of this definition of war is that it does not require the participation of states. Similarly, Michael Howard defines war as 'all armed conflict between political entities, whether or not these are or claim to be recognised as sovereign states'.[42] Thus, Kaldor goes on to write: 'The most important difference between new wars and earlier wars is that new wars do not presuppose the existence of states.'[43]

State control and state formation conflicts can perhaps be considered 'modern' wars because they involve disputes over state power, so that the 'modern' state as an authoritative and sovereign political unit is still central to defining them. State failure conflicts, on the other hand, are 'post-modern' precisely because the state's role as a sovereign political entity with a monopoly over the organised use of violence is being challenged, diminished and perhaps even superseded.

Kloos, for example, refers to the Sri Lanka civil war as 'a fairly typical example of the kind of civil war flowing from the construction of a colonial state and failing nation-building after independence'. As such, he distinguishes it from 'civil wars' in the context of state failure or state disintegration, in which 'sub-state minorities' bypass weak or failing state structures to operate directly in the global arena.[44]

As with contemporary armed conflicts more generally, state failure wars occur for a wide variety of reasons, including external economic pressures, historical legacy, internal corruption or incompetence, and the increased role of identity politics. In some cases, modern state structures have been only weakly grafted on to more traditional forms of social organisation, particularly in post-colonial situations where territorial boundaries and a centralised administration have been arbitrarily imposed by the departing imperial powers. This is true of nomadic or pastoralist societies such as Somalia or Afghanistan. Both are notorious recent instances of state failure, where local warlords have repeatedly challenged and undermined attempts to develop a modern, centralised state. In the case of Somalia, the 'introduction of the state by the colonial powers' was a 'source of unrest, causing friction between modern governance and ancient traditional social practices'.[45]

According to Auvinen and Kivimäki, for example:

Groups larger than clans did not have much influence in Somali culture of power [sic], reflecting the nature of moving pastoral production ... Prior to European colonization, Somalis did not constitute a state. It was not possible for moving groups of people to create wider stable institutions of cooperation and order and thus the emergence of stable state institutions was not feasible. This is one of the reasons the Somali state remained weak in the post-colonial context.

Furthermore, pre-colonial clan loyalties have remained stronger than any allegiance to the Somali state, which contributed to its disintegration in the context of civil war and famine in the early 1990s.[46] The state was seen primarily as 'the main means of political competition for personal wealth in Somalia rather than being a vehicle for the maximization of public welfare'.[47]

Somalia, in other words, is 'a society in which people identify themselves as members of clans rather than as Somalis'.[48] In addition to contributing to state failure, clan loyalties have been used as 'mechanisms of mobilization' in violent conflicts in Somalia, so that 'much of the killing after the state collapse has been related to "clan-cleansing"'.[49]

Kaldor in particular emphasises the importance of 'identity politics' as a distinguishing characteristic of 'new wars', where identification with cultural labels defined in terms of ethnicity, language or religion supersedes explicitly political goals connected to state power.[50] Similarly, Latham suggests that the era of post-modern war is characterised by 'the simultaneous emergence of both inclusive "cosmopolitan" forms of collective identity and more fragmented and particularistic "imagined communities" based on "ethnicity", race or religion', as distinct from national identities associated with the nation-state.[51] And Rob McRae argues that such 'ethnically-based violence and aggression is identity-affirming in the face of insecurity and fear, i.e., when traditional social structures break down',[52] or when the state loses its capacity to protect the safety and wellbeing of its citizens. In other words, identity politics both contributes to and results from state failure.

Such labelling, which is 'inherently exclusive and separatist', also helps explain the deliberate targeting of civilians in such wars.[53] The result, however, is that the government loses its control over organized violence within a clearly defined geographical territory, a crucial characteristic of the modern state.

Other analysts, on the other hand, claim that such 'identity politics' are more often than not used as a convenient pretext or justification for the predatory or criminal activities of the armed gangs that operate in the absence of an effective state:

> Identity, ethnicity, nationalism, civilization, culture, and religion proved to be more nearly an excuse, pretext, or general organizing principle for their predations rather than an independent cause of them ... When governments become weak, it is likely (almost by definition) that criminal activity will increase, and sometimes the resulting criminality will be organized enough to look like war.[54]

The predatory nature of the armed groups involved in such wars, because they are concerned with the pursuit of private gain rather than the public goals or 'national interest' associated with the state, means that they 'often do not even seem to have an "endgame" of winning the conflict and returning to peace'.[55] Thus, the 'privatisation' of war refers not merely to those who engage in the use of armed force, but also to the purposes for which it is used.

Furthermore, the more conventional distinction between civil and international war becomes blurred in the context of post-modern wars because of the disintegration of state structures, including territorial boundaries, and the increased involvement of nonstate actors, for whom such boundaries may not be relevant. Kaldor argues, for example, that 'external support takes a variety of forms' in such conflicts, including 'diaspora elements' as well as 'transnational commercial networks', both legal and illegal.[56] Thus, such wars become both global and local, or externally as well as internally driven by a variety of nonstate actors.[57]

The so-called 'war on terror', with the US government and Al Qaeda as its principal antagonists, conforms to many of the features of post-modern war, as Richard Falk suggests. 'Both Al Qaeda and the US seem committed to waging borderless wars on a global scale.' Furthermore, they are not engaged in conventional state control or state formation wars, that is, they are not 'engaged in a civil war for control of a state, or waging some sort of self-determination struggle'. Finally, according to Falk: 'Neither adversary is a sovereign state in the normally understood sense.' The US 'is a kind of global state that claims command of the oceans and space, as well as maintaining military bases in more than sixty countries'. Al Qaeda, on the other hand, 'is an amorphous, dispersed, secretive network that is operative in as many as sixty states'.[58]

The defining feature of post-modern war, then, is that it occurs in the context of the diminished capacity of sovereign states to control the use of armed force or organised violence both internally and internationally. Furthermore, as we have seen from the examples of Sri Lanka and Somalia, state formation and state control conflicts can easily degenerate into state failure (or post-modern) conflicts, especially where identity politics or external factors play a significant role. Thus, many contemporary armed conflicts are perhaps a type of 'constitutive war' (to use Latham's phrase), marking a transition from modern to post-modern forms of war.

Post-modern war may also incorporate significant instances of 'asymmetric warfare', or armed conflict between groups with vastly unequal military power, particularly since the events of 11 September 2001 (and the subsequent military response). One possible example of such asymmetric warfare might be the current intifada in the West Bank, the Gaza strip and

Israel. So-called 'suicide bombers', then, might be viewed as the weapons of the weak, at least in conventional military and perhaps political terms, in the context of such asymmetric warfare. According to Paul Rogers, 'trends suggest that seemingly invulnerable states, however powerful and wealthy they may be, have innate weaknesses that can be readily exploited in an era of asymmetric warfare'.[59]

Furthermore, such asymmetric warfare, including the activities of Al Qaeda and other transnational nonstate terrorist networks, represents perhaps the implications of state failure to retain control over organised violence on a global or international scale. US strategy since the September 11th attacks, on the other hand, partly involves a conventional state security response in the form of the war against the Taliban regime in Afghanistan followed by the war against Iraq. In the case of the latter in particular, we have seen a return to war as an instrument of foreign policy in the absence of either a 'balance of power' or the effective rule of law at the international level. In other words, if post-modern wars signify a failure of domestic order, in the form of the state's control over organised violence, the return to more conventional international war seems to signify a failure of a state-based international order, in the form of multi-lateralism and respect for international law. This is further demonstrated by the US administration's support for 'pre-emptive war' and its search for 'full spectrum dominance', as espoused through the so-called Bush doctrine on US foreign policy.

## IV. COSMOPOLITAN RESPONSES TO POST-MODERN WAR

Realist, internationalist and cosmopolitan theories of international politics each suggest their own responses to the problem of post-modern war. The realist will look to state power in the form of the use of overwhelming military force as the most effective way of eliminating the sources of threat associated with post-modern wars. The US military pursuit of Al Qaeda in Afghanistan and the various resistance groups in Iraq epitomises this type of action. These examples reveal the limited effectiveness of conventional military action against such opponents in the context of asymmetrical conflict, however, not to mention their tremendous costs in terms of civilian casualties.

There is also a normative component to the realist response to post-modern war, however, represented by a commitment to state-building as the best way to mitigate state failure as the trigger for such conflicts. Such state-building involves an emphasis on democratisation, including the formal mechanisms of representative government, as well as good governance, including an effective legal system and an efficient and honest civil service. Again, this focus on state-building is revealed in the international community's approach to post-Taliban Afghanistan.

This emphasis on state-building suggests that post-modern war is primarily a problem of domestic civil disorder, or the absence of the effective rule of state-enforced law. The armed gangs as well as those in control of the state apparatus (including the military) perpetrating the violence and the human rights abuses in the context of these 'wars' often operate on the basis of criminal greed rather than to represent the interests of the civilian population or to further any clearly identifiable political objectives. As John Mueller says, 'many of these "low-intensity wars" seem more nearly to be high-intensity crime'.[60]

The implication is that societies experiencing such conflicts must replicate the processes of state-building begun in Europe centuries previously in an effort to subdue and control such anarchic violence.[61] In other words, such conflicts resemble pre-modern wars because of the privatised and fragmented nature of the violence associated with them.

On the other hand, these conflicts can be distinguished from the problems of civil disorder associated with pre-modern wars because, although they are in some senses highly local in their immediate causes and effects, they can also be highly global because of the range of actors and interests involved. The processes of globalisation that can produce economic and social pressures resulting in the weakening and fragmentation of states also make it difficult to contain the ramifications and consequences of 'internal conflicts' within state boundaries.

> Globalization, which ironically leads also to the globalization of fragmentation itself, internationalizes such conflicts … which, in different circumstances, may have had only a local or regional significance and effect. Today, internal wars are neither politically nor even legally speaking any more internal affairs of states in the territory of which they occur. Moreover, more often than not even internal wars extend to territories of more than one state and thereby become internationalized.[62]

In other words, although they can be highly local and fragmented, post-modern wars are influenced or affected by a wide variety of international or global economic and political factors, which the modern, sovereign state on its own may not be able to deal with adequately. An exclusive focus on state-building and domestic order may not be sufficient to deal with the causes and consequences of post-modern war.

Internationalists, however, can incorporate a global dimension into their response to post-modern war, through their emphasis on international law and multilateral organisations, especially the UN. Thus, the realist focus on state-building and domestic order is supplemented by these two components of 'global governance', which can provide the mechanisms and resources for dealing with the international dimension of post-modern conflicts.

Furthermore, global governance, with its emphasis on such norms as the sovereign equality of states in the context of international law, for example, can act as some sort of restraint on concentrations of power either regionally or internationally, epitomised currently by the unprecedented dominance or hegemony of the US, and related to that, the role of Israel in the Middle East. Thus, global governance can act, at least in theory, as a counterbalance to the disparities of power at the heart of asymmetric armed conflicts by providing an additional avenue for disaffected groups to pursue their claims or grievances.

Finally, cosmopolitanism may want to emphasise the significance of shared norms and values (such as a commitment to human rights and open dialogue) as a vital component of any response to post-modern wars, particularly where these involve the fragmentation of inclusive political communities when confronted with exclusive expressions of identity (race, ethnicity or nationality, for instance). Furthermore, transnational civil society, comprised of human rights, environmental, peace and development NGOs (nongovernmental organisations), for example, is perhaps the clearest embodiment of these cosmopolitan values.

In other words, state-building, global governance and transnational civil society could all be seen as complementary elements of an effective response to post-modern armed conflict. This could take the form of a Kantian emphasis on the three levels of *recht* (moral and legal rights): domestic, international and cosmopolitan as the basis of 'perpetual', or at least institutionalised, peace.

On the other hand, transnational civil society may provide some sort of cosmopolitan alternative to the concentrations of military power associated with state structures or even state-based multilateral organisations. These structures or organisations may provide short-term coercive responses to problems of civil disorder and international conflict, but they ultimately rely on the use or at least the threat of armed force and violence for their immediate effectiveness. Transnational civil society, with its cosmopolitan values, may provide a necessary response to the 'Hobbesian dilemma' of the state, according to which the concentration of coercive political power it requires to protect its citizens can also be used against them as well as to threaten the security of the citizens of other states. The 'human security' paradigm, discussed in the next chapter, may provide a cosmopolitan alternative to the problems posed by conventional 'state security' as a response to contemporary armed conflict, or post-modern war.

## NOTES

1. Mueller, 'Policing the Remnants of War', p. 508.
2. Project Ploughshares, *Armed Conflicts Report 1997*, p. 4.
3. Ibid. pp. 4, 6.
4. Ibid. p. 6.
5. Zahar, 'Protégés, Clients, Cannon Fodder', p. 107.
6. Latham, 'Warfare Transformed', p. 256.
7. Smith, 'Guerillas in the mist', p. 19.
8. Zahar, 'Protégés, Clients, Cannon Fodder', p. 107.
9. Kaldor, 'A Cosmopolitan Response to New Wars', p. 507.
10. Goodhand and Hulme, 'From wars to complex political emergencies', p. 17.
11. Zahar, 'Protégés, Clients, Cannon Fodder', p. 121.
12. Auvinen and Kivimäki, 'Somalia: The Struggle for Resources', p. 210.
13. Keen, 'Sudan: Conflict and Rationality', p. 220.
14. Ibid. p. 231.
15. Goodhand and Hulme, 'From wars to complex political emergencies', pp. 16–17.
16. Harris and Lewis, 'Armed Conflict in Developing Countries', p. 9.
17. See Nissan, 'Historical Context', p. 18.
18. Fernando, 'Root Causes of Ethnic Conflict', p. 20.
19. Nissan, 'Historical Context', p. 12.
20. Kloos, 'A turning point?', p. 186.
21. Nissan, 'Historical Context', p. 17.
22. Fernando, 'Root Causes of Ethnic Conflict', p. 29.
23. Nissan, 'Historical Context', p. 17.
24. See both Fernando, 'Root Causes of Ethnic Conflict' and Kloos, 'A turning point?'
25. Fernando, 'Root Causes of Ethnic Conflict', p. 28.
26. Ibid. p. 19.
27. See, for example, Nissan, 'Historical Context', pp. 17–18.
28. See ibid. p. 19.
29. Kloos, 'A turning point?', pp. 189–90.
30. Saravanamuttu, 'Sri Lanka', p. 131.
31. Kloos, 'A turning point?', p. 190.
32. Saravanamuttu, 'Sri Lanka', p. 132.
33. Bullion, 'Dreaming of a War-Free Future', p. 27.
34. See Kaldor, *New and Old Wars*.
35. Latham, 'Warfare Transformed', p. 247.
36. Ibid. p. 249.
37. Ibid. p. 251.
38. Ibid. p. 252.
39. Ibid. p. 263.
40. Bull, *The Anarchical Society*, p. 185.
41. Kaldor, 'Introduction', pp. 7–8.
42. Howard, 'When Are Wars Decisive?', p. 126.
43. Kaldor, 'Introduction', p. 9.
44. Kloos, 'A turning point?', p. 194.
45. Auvinen and Kivimäki, 'Somalia: The Struggle for Resources', p. 207.
46. Ibid. pp. 195–6.
47. Ibid. p. 206.
48. Ibid. p. 196.

49. Ibid. pp. 196–7.
50. Kaldor, 'Introduction', p. 11.
51. Latham, 'Warfare Transformed', pp. 254–5.
52. McRae, 'Conclusion: International Relations and the New Diplomacy', p. 258.
53. Kaldor, 'Introduction', p. 12.
54. Mueller, 'Policing the Remnants of War', p. 508. See also Mueller, 'The Banality of "Ethnic War"', pp. 42–70.
55. Zack-Williams, 'The Forgotten Realities of Contemporary Africa', p. 118.
56. Kaldor, 'Introduction', p. 14.
57. Ibid. p. 18.
58. Falk, 'A New Gandhian Moment?', p. 8.
59. Rogers, *Losing Control*, p. 112.
60. Mueller, 'Policing the Remnants of War', p. 509.
61. See ibid. pp. 510–11.
62. Müllerson, '*Jus Ad Bellum*', p. 155.

CHAPTER 8

# HUMAN SECURITY, HUMAN RIGHTS AND HUMAN DEVELOPMENT

The concept of human security emphasises the safety and wellbeing of ordinary human beings rather than the narrow focus on state or national security that has formed the basis of international relations in recent decades. As such, it incorporates a range of issues, including human rights, humanitarian law and a broad vision of 'sustainable human development'. The emphasis on the needs and rights of individuals in the context of humanity as a whole, rather than as citizens of particular states or members of exclusive political communities, highlights the cosmopolitan component of the norms and values behind a commitment to human security. It is also important to maintain the distinction between the 'soft power' of cooperation and dialogue required to achieve the objectives of human security, and the 'hard', military power associated with the defence of state or national security.

## I. ASPECTS OF HUMAN SECURITY

The central difference between human security and a more traditional concept of security, particularly within a 'realist' interpretation of international politics, is its focus on individual human beings, rather than the state, as the object (or referent) of security. As Fen Osler Hampson says: 'In the human security "paradigm" ... individuals and communities of individuals rather than governments or "states" are the primary point of reference.'[1] The focus of human security, as distinct from state or national security, is on the concerns of ordinary people seeking safety and wellbeing in their daily lives.

The value of the state, and the importance of its security, rests on its usefulness as an instrument for protecting 'the rights and physical security of the individual'.[2] In other words, the state (and the security of the state) has a purely instrumental value based upon its capacity to provide genuine human security for individuals. As Bill McSweeney points out, the difficulty with the 'primacy of the state in the political

111

science tradition' is precisely that, in effect, 'the means have become the end'.[3] If one adopts a human security perspective, on the other hand, then: 'Ontologically, the state is an instrument of security, and human individuals are its subject.' Furthermore, this implies that 'the collective good' cannot 'be subsumed under the needs and requirements of the organization of the state'.[4]

The United Nations Development Programme (UNDP) *Human Development Report* for 1994, which is widely credited as the origin of recent serious concern about this view of security, identifies seven main categories of threat to human security. Only one form of threat, 'threats from other states (war)' in one of these seven categories, 'physical violence', corresponds to the central concern of conventional state or national security. Other categories of threat (with their corresponding dimension of human security) include economic, food, health and environmental concerns.[5]

The report also divides threats to human security into two types: chronic and immediate. Thus, the report refers to two aspects of human security: 'safety from chronic threats such as hunger, disease and repression' and 'protection from sudden and harmful disruptions in the patterns of daily life'.[6] Human security, as distinct from state security, is a holistic and inclusive concept covering the full range of threats to human well-being and survival. In the words of Dunne and Wheeler, 'the human security discourse recognizes the multidimensionality of the sources of harm'.[7]

Proponents of human security sometimes argue that the state must still be seen as one of the principal instruments for achieving the security of individuals, in line with conventional Western political theory.[8] They also claim, however, that the state on its own is no longer capable of providing such security, so that state security is no longer synonymous with or a guarantee of individual security. King and Murray point out that 'even successful examples of territorial security', as the prime goal of national security policy, 'do not necessarily ensure the security of citizens within a state', partly because so many threats, such as 'environmental degradation and natural disasters', transcend state boundaries, and partly because state behaviour itself can be a source of threat to its citizens.[9] 'This personalization of security entails a recognition that the interests of individual human beings are distinct from, and might even conflict with, those of states.'[10]

A focus on human security must recognise that the state itself can constitute a threat, and perhaps even the greatest threat, to individual human beings, as we have seen so many times during the last century or so. Thus, states, far from protecting the fundamental rights of their citizens, are sometimes the source of the worst human rights abuses, in the form of genocide and the systematic torture and 'disappearance' of large numbers of human beings. The UNDP explicitly identifies 'threats from the state (physical torture)' as one form of physical violence that threatens human security.[11]

It is because states can often provide only limited protection for individual human beings, and are sometimes a source of threat rather than protection, that the traditional or conventional concept of state security must be replaced or superseded by the broader or more accurate concept of human security. 'The focus must broaden from the state to the security of people – to human security.'[12]

The human security paradigm focuses on protecting individual human beings from threats to their survival, wellbeing or basic rights, although the recent Commission on Human Security provides a positive as well as a negative component in its more expansive definition. 'Human security focuses on shielding people from critical and pervasive threats and empowering them to take charge of their lives. It demands creating genuine opportunities for people to live in safety and dignity and earn their livelihood.'[13]

The Commission on Human Security was established in 2001 at the initiative of the Government of Japan in response to the call by UN Secretary-General Kofi Annan at the UN Millennium Summit the previous year for the international community to focus on securing the twin goals of 'freedom from fear' and 'freedom from want'.[14] As such, its two broad areas of concern were 'human insecurities resulting from conflict and violence', and 'links between human security and development'.[15]

The Commission was 'independent of the United Nations, governments, and international organizations', although it maintained close contact with the UN and had the support of Annan.[16] It was co-chaired by Sadako Ogata, former UN High Commissioner for Refugees, and Amartya Sen, Nobel laureate in economics. The Commission presented its final report to Annan on 1 May 2003. The report includes specific policy conclusions and recommendations for action in such areas as 'protecting people from the proliferation of arms', 'working to provide minimum living standards everywhere' and 'according high priority to ensuring universal access to basic health care' in response to its multidimensional interpretation of human security.

Similarly, Hampson refers to 'the individual's physical security and protection of basic liberties' as well as 'minimal conditions for human welfare and survival' as the key components of human security.[17] These components can in turn be linked to his three interpretations of or approaches to implementing human security.

## II. THREE APPROACHES TO HUMAN SECURITY

In his book *Madness in the Multitude: Human Security and World Disorder*, Hampson outlines three different understandings of human security. The first concerns threats to the fundamental human rights of individuals, and is 'anchored in the rule of law and treaty-based solutions to human security'. He refers to the second as humanitarian, because it is primarily concerned with threats arising from war and armed conflict, and makes 'an important moral distinction between combatants and noncombatants'. The third, and perhaps 'most expansive definition of human security is what might be termed the "sustainable human development" view', associated with the 1994 UNDP *Human Development Report*.[18]

The rights-based approach to human security focuses on the denial of basic rights, the absence of the rule of law and undemocratic systems of governance as the main threats to human security.[19] As such, it 'has its origins in liberal democratic theory and the foundations of the modern democratic state'.[20] The Commission on Human Security incorporates this view when it states: 'Respecting human rights are [*sic*] at the core of protecting human security.'[21] The UNDP also recognised this as one of the dimensions of its broad understanding of human security: 'One of the most important aspects of human security is that people should be able to live in a society that honours their basic rights.'[22] Conversely: 'If security is defined as protection from harm, then it is clear that the infringement of fundamental rights signifies the presence of insecurity.'[23]

The link between human rights and security is an explicit part of the international human rights regime that has developed since 1945, according to Dunne and Wheeler.[24] They claim, for example, that human security can be connected to a range of both economic and social rights as well as civil and political rights through its focus on both human wellbeing and 'subsistence' and on 'security from violence'.[25] The reference to the fulfilment of human rights as the purpose of an international order based on international peace and security in the UN Charter and the Universal Declaration of Human Rights (UDHR) represents 'a considerable challenge to the traditional realist paradigm', with its emphasis on the priority or supremacy of state sovereignty, because 'the way in which a state behaved towards its own citizens' became a legitimate subject of international concern.[26] Multilateral institutions, and the UN in particular, become significant as the means by which human security, embodied in international norms and in international law, becomes implemented.

According to Hampson, the second approach to human security has traditionally focused on humanitarian law and humanitarian relief, through 'securing the moral and legal rights of noncombatants in war or situations of violent conflict and on providing emergency assistance to those in dire need'. Humanitarian law makes a clear distinction between combatants and noncombatants. It prohibits directly targeting noncombatants, but also increasingly requires military antagonists to 'carry out military operations in such a way that the risk of harming civilians' is limited. The connection between humanitarian law and the just war principles of noncombatant immunity (or 'discrimination') and 'due care' are discussed in Chapter 5. These principles are expressed in the Hague Conventions of 1899 and 1907 and the Geneva Conventions of 1949.[27] Interpreted in human security terms, this reflects 'the paradigm shift for international security: from a concern with protecting and enhancing the security of states, to the protection and security of civilians'.[28]

Hampson argues that, since the 1990s, this second approach to human security also includes a concern with 'preventive and post-conflict peace-building', suggesting that it 'sees a need to go beyond the provision of emergency and humanitarian relief in war-torn societies and conflict settings by addressing the *underlying* causes of conflict and violence'.[29] The purpose of such peacebuilding, according to the Canadian govern-ment, 'is to enhance the indigenous capacity of a society to manage con-flict without violence'.[30] As such, peacebuilding is 'highly interventionist', involving as it does attempts to alter the fundamental political, social and economic structures of a country or society in order to enhance its capacity for human security.[31] Peacebuilding as an expression of the human security agenda and the cosmopolitan values with which it is associated is discussed in Chapter 10.

Another recent focus of this approach to human security concerns types of weapons that form a particular threat to civilians or noncomba-tants during war or armed conflict, such as landmines or small arms and light weapons (SALWs).[32] Thus, Lloyd Axworthy, former Minister for External Affairs of Canada, claims that the Ottawa Convention of 1997 banning antipersonnel landmines 'was the first concrete, public expression of the human security agenda'.[33]

This humanitarian human security agenda requires more than develop-ing or erecting the legal infrastructure for protecting noncombatants during armed conflict and war. It also requires compliance with inter-national law on the part of states and other warring groups. The recent UN Secretary-General's report on *Protection of Civilians in Armed Conflict* (September 1999), for example, 'was clear that the legal foundations for protecting civilians are largely in place, and what is lacking is adherence to international human rights, humanitarian, and refugee law'.[34]

The third approach to human security, 'sustainable human develop-ment', moves beyond the concern with war and armed conflict as specific threats to noncombatants, to a much broader examination of the whole 'array of threats that jeopardize human survival and well-being'. In this sense, it corresponds to the original definition of human security provided by the UNDP in its 1994 *Human Development Report*.

Furthermore, this understanding of human security challenges the traditional realist emphasis on state security not merely because of its focus on the wellbeing of individual human beings, but also because 'those threats considered to be the most relevant – such as environmental degradation and population growth', transcend national boundaries and must be considered in a global context.[35] Thus, both multilateral institutions (such as the UN) and civil society organisations (such as development, environmental and human rights NGOs), which also transcend state boundaries, play a special role in realising this concept of human security.[36]

These wider threats to human security are sometimes categorised as examples of 'structural violence', as distinct from the direct, physical violence of war and armed conflict. Problems such as poverty and inequality can result in significant harm to the wellbeing of billions of human beings worldwide. As the Commission on Human Security points out, for example: 'More than 800,000 people a year lose their lives to [physical] violence. About 2.8 billion suffer from poverty, ill health, illiteracy and other maladies.'[37]

Unlike direct violence, however, such threats to human security are supposedly built into global economic and political structures, and are not the directly intended result of deliberate human agency.

> In the human security conception, threats must be reckoned as both direct and indirect; they arise from identifiable sources, such as other states or non-state actors of various kinds, and also from structural sources – that is, from relations of power at various levels from the family upward to the global economy. In the latter case, threats are not easily traceable to the intentions of any one or more actors and may be the unintended consequences of others' actions or even inactions.[38]

Transnational corporations or international bodies responsible for trade policy, for example, do not set out to impoverish human beings living in large parts of the developing world, although this may be an unintended consequence of their policies. Categorising such problems as a form of violence, furthermore, perhaps makes it more credible to refer to them as threats to human security as well as failures of socio-economic development. Human security, in other words, requires the elimination or at least the amelioration of structural as well as direct violence. Even if these problems of social and economic development are not analysed as forms of 'structural violence', however, they can still be incorporated into the human security agenda because of its general concern with the full range of obstacles or threats to human wellbeing and survival.

Although this approach to human security moves beyond a specific focus on war and armed conflict, it also recognises an intimate link between conflict and some of these wider concerns, such as poverty. For example, 'eight of the 10 countries that scored lowest' on the UNDP's Human Development Index (HDI), 'and eight out of 10 countries with the lowest GNP per capita, have experienced civil wars in the recent past'.[39] Thus, poverty and armed conflict must be tackled together as threats to human security in its broadest sense.

Various UN agencies and initiatives represent perhaps the most coherent attempt to formulate and implement this approach to human security, in particular the UNDP through its characteristic human development framework. The Commission on Human Security is another recent attempt to pursue this broad human security agenda. The Commission states explicitly: 'Achieving human security requires ... undertaking efforts to address the full range of critical and pervasive threats facing people.' These threats involve those derived from war and armed conflict, but also those associated with human migration (including displacement within and across national boundaries), economic insecurity (including poverty) and health (such as HIV/AIDS and other infectious diseases).[40]

Recent efforts by some UN agencies (particularly UNICEF and the UNDP) and NGOs to implement a 'human rights based approach to development' provide perhaps a synthesis of Hampson's first and third human security paradigms. At the heart of this approach is the suggestion that the substantive articles of international human rights treaties, particularly the UDHR and the two covenants on civil and political rights and on economic, social and cultural rights (that is, the International Bill of Rights), can provide the basis for formulating and implementing detailed development strategies embodying the objectives of 'sustainable human development'. Mary Robinson has referred to 'rights-based approaches to development' as 'the operational expression of the link between human rights and development'.[41] It also provides a connection between the international law dimension of human security (especially human rights law) and the broad social and economic goals of its sustainable human development dimension.

The central principle of the rights-based approach to development is that development is the process by which people realise their basic human rights. Furthermore, these rights are embodied or encapsulated in international human rights treaties or instruments. The most important of these are the UDHR and the two 1966 covenants, supplemented by the UN Declaration of the Right to Development (1986), as well as international treaties covering specific rights issues, particularly the Convention on the Elimination of Discrimination Against Women (CEDAW), the Convention on the Rights of the Child (CRC) and the Convention Against Torture (CAT). Many of the rights contained in these instruments underpin the international development targets agreed by aid donors at various fora, including the UN's special Millennium Summit.

It has been claimed that the human rights approach to development reflects best practice in sustainable human development. It can be argued more directly that the rights-based approach offers the best way to achieve the goals of human development, because specific human rights encapsulate or embody particular human development targets. For instance, the core human development indicators in the UNDP annual *Human Development Report*, life expectancy, literacy and level of income, can be connected to basic human rights to the highest attainable standard of physical and mental health, education, and so on.

There is a danger of course that in attempting to humanise security through attaching it to a wider range of economic and social development goals one could also 'securitise' development. Development assistance, for instance, could be channelled towards funding more conventional military activity in order to deal more robustly with armed conflicts and political violence that are preventing or undoing attempts at social and political development. There is a risk, for example, that the new African Peace Facility aimed at training indigenous African peacekeepers operating through or on behalf of the African Union will be partly funded out of the European Union development budget. Plan Colombia represents another attempt to couple military with development objectives, with the US funding the former and the EU being asked to fund the latter. And there has been a dangerous blurring of military operations and humanitarian assistance in post-Taliban Afghanistan in the context of the so-called Provincial Reconstruction Teams (PRTs) of the US military. It is for this reason that the human security approach ought to be seen perhaps as a genuine alternative to the conventional military response to state security issues, rather than as somehow supplementary to it.

## III. HUMAN SECURITY AND THE USE OF ARMED FORCE

It can be argued that human security (as distinct from state security), whether understood as the defence of fundamental human rights, the protection of noncombatants during wartime or the pursuit of a 'sustainable human development agenda', is best realised through utilising a wide variety of nonmilitary (or nonviolent) rather than military methods. The

UNDP, for example, argued that human security is an integrative rather than a defensive concept, unlike territorial or state security, and for this reason it 'cannot be brought about through force, with armies standing against armies'.[42]

All three interpretations or understandings of human security can be pursued by noncoercive means, such as diplomacy or other efforts at international cooperation, or what is sometimes referred to as 'soft power'.[43] Thus, Rob McRae claims that the human security agenda 'is particularly susceptible to the exercise of soft power, to the extent that it appeals for support and attracts adherents, rather than coercing allegiance'.[44] This soft power approach characterised the attainment of the Ottawa Convention on landmines, for example.

Military action, on the other hand, is recognised as a significant threat to human security under all three approaches. It represents an obvious threat to such fundamental human rights as the right to life. The central purpose of the humanitarian approach is to contain the threats to human security arising in the context of the use of armed force. Finally, the use of armed force can undermine or threaten the social and economic conditions necessary to achieve sustainable human development.

As Kanti Bajpai points out, this emphasis on the 'soft power' of diplomacy and international cooperation, as distinct from the 'hard' coercive power of military force, is another way of distinguishing the human security approach from a conventional realist or neorealist understanding of security. According to Bajpai, 'in the traditional conception of security, hard or military power is central. In the human security conception, soft power or the power of persuasion is central.' Force is at best 'a secondary instrument' because force 'is not very effective in dealing with the multifarious threats to personal safety and freedom' encompassed by human security. Force should certainly not be used in pursuit of narrow state or national interest, but only for 'the more cosmopolitan goal of managing human security threats' through enforcing international law, for example.[45]

The 'war on terror' initiated by the Bush administration in response to the Al Qaeda attacks of 11 September 2001, on the other hand, involves the inappropriate use of conventional military methods associated with state or national security to deal with a specific type of threat to personal or individual security. In the case of the invasion and occupation of Iraq in particular, this has only exacerbated these threats, especially for Iraqi civilians. Furthermore, the military invasion and occupation of Iraq has itself become one of the main threats to the wider range of human security concerns associated with the daily life of ordinary Iraqis, such as access to food, income, health care, and so on. More generally, it has undermined multilateralism and international law as the institutional framework for attaining human security, especially in 'post-war' situations.

The human security approach, as distinct from realism or neorealism, emphasises cooperation rather than competition as a viable and indeed vital characteristic of international politics. States or governments must collaborate with each other through multilateral institutions, and with 'non-governmental organizations and other agencies in civil society', in response to threats to human security. Such cooperation is best achieved through the exercise of soft power, in the form of diplomacy, dialogue and the dissemination of ideas and information.[46]

## IV. HUMAN SECURITY AND COSMOPOLITANISM

The human security paradigm suggests that each human being has a value that transcends state boundaries, and furthermore that individual human beings can form some sort of community for the purposes of human security that exists independently of states and their political and territorial boundaries. Thus, the 'referent object' of human security is the 'individuals who constitute humanity as a whole'.[47]

Such a community can be considered cosmopolitan in the sense that it includes all human beings, united by common or shared values, whether these are reflected in fundamental human rights, a shared respect for human life or the goals of 'sustainable human development'. Bajpai claims that the 'human security conception ... is universal, i.e., applicable to any society in the world'.[48]

Similarly, the UNDP identifies universality and indivisibility as essential characteristics of human security. 'It is relevant to people everywhere, in rich nations and poor.'[49] Furthermore: 'It acknowledges the universalism of life claims ... It is embedded in a notion of solidarity among people.'[50] Global human security is indivisible because 'when human security is under threat anywhere, it can affect people everywhere'.[51]

Hampson suggests that 'advocates of human security ... believe that although human beings may be divided by language, culture, ethnicity, religion, and political beliefs, they also share many things in common'.[52] Similarly, the Commission on Human Security concludes that human security requires 'a global human identity while respecting the freedom of individuals to have diverse identities and affiliations'.[53]

Thus, the object of security becomes not merely the individual human being, but also humanity as a whole as the collection of all such individuals. The state is an intermediate political instrument, but by no means the only one, for achieving such collective human security. 'The point of reference or "object" of security is not the nation-state and its territory but individual people in their daily activities, wherever they live, and humanity as a collective body in which all individuals are members.'[54] There is an intimate link between the security of each individual and the security of humanity as a whole.

All three interpretations of human security depend upon a sense of shared humanity as well as a shared, cosmopolitan set of values. This strongly normative base is also reflected in the human security emphasis upon soft, or normative, power. This focus upon values, and specifically cosmopolitan values, rather than interests, and specifically national interests, is an important point of vulnerability for the human security agenda, since it must account for any conflict that arises between supposedly cosmopolitan values and perceived special interests. The opposition of the United States government, and of other powers with a vested interest in the international arms trade such as China and Russia, to the landmines treaty is an important case in point. As McRae suggests: 'Domestically, human security depends on strong public support for an agenda that has more to do with values than national interests.'[55] US refusal to ratify a number of human rights conventions, and other international treaties, also demonstrates the clash between perceived national interest and the norms or values underlying a human security approach to international politics.

Another vulnerability associated with the cosmopolitan dimension of human security is its focus on abstract individuals, outside the context of the specific communities (ethnicity, nationality, and so on) that help to form their identities, defined ethically through supposedly universal principles. Such principles may in fact reflect Western perspectives, on human rights for example, including of course the focus on the individual as the ultimate source or locus of value.

Hampson distinguishes four different positions concerning 'which international actors or institutions are best able to deliver' human security as an international public good.[56] These positions are civil society cosmopolitanism, liberal multilateral institutionalism, hegemonic minilateralism and middle-power multilateralism.[57] Of these four, he identifies 'civil society, especially non-governmental organizations, and broadly-based social movements' with an explicitly cosmopolitan position, linking the individual directly with the concerns of humanity as a whole.[58] McRae agrees that 'global civil society will by its very nature take the individual (here and now) as the starting point for any issue', so that the 'human security agenda ... may yet be regarded as the first step toward a truly postmodern internationalism that puts our shared humanity at its core'.[59]

Dunne and Wheeler, on the other hand, argue that 'the project of unifying human rights and security requires ... an alliance of states and transnational civil society cooperating to achieve security for common humanity'.[60] While they are impressed by the impact of transnational civil society on the evolving human rights regime, they also point out some of the limits of NGO action in the world of power politics. They warn too against the assumption that civil society organisations will always be on the side of the angels, or even operate on the basis of shared underlying values or norms.[61] 'We should not be surprised that transnational forces can be reactionary as well as emancipatory: contradictory normative tendencies are at work in all forms of social organization.'[62] In accordance with their 'multidimensional approach to agency', they stress that NGOs and governments need not always be antagonists, and that 'moral boundaries have frequently been widened when state actors and global civil society have pulled in the same direction'.[63] The landmines treaty, for example, was achieved through the cooperation of 'middle powers', such as Canada and Norway, with NGOs such as the Nobel prize-winning International Campaign to Ban Landmines operating, significantly, outside conventional UN processes.

Furthermore, if the protection and fulfilment of human rights is an integral part of human security, then ensuring that human rights norms are incorporated into domestic and international state policy and practice will go a long way towards meeting the requirements of human security. As Bertrand Ramcharan says, 'building strong human rights institutions at the national level is what will ensure that human rights are protected and advanced in a sustained manner in the long run'.[64] States, as the nexus of political and legal jurisdiction in a given society, have a particular role to play in entrenching and promoting human rights and hence human security both nationally and internationally.

In other words, states and state-based multilateral organisations can become vehicles for the implementation of the cosmopolitan human security agenda. Or, as Hataley and Nossal put it, 'the human security agenda, if it is to be taken seriously, suggests that the state embracing it should organize itself in a way to be able to implement its commitment to the safety of ordinary people in other places'.[65]

The human security paradigm focuses on the safety and wellbeing of individuals, and of humanity as a whole, rather than the security of the state, as the object or referent of security in the context of international politics. The three different interpretations of the human security agenda suggested by Hampson can be best achieved by nonmilitary or nonviolent methods, as distinct from the conventional suggestion that military (or 'hard') power is the ultimate guarantee of security.

There is also a strong link between human security and cosmopolitanism, because of its emphasis on the individual as a member of a universal moral community. The strongly normative foundations of human security do suggest a number of problems or questions concerning the conflict or contradiction between cosmopolitan values and national or other special interests in the context of international politics, as well as the possible cultural (that is, Western) bias implicit in such values. Thus, the human security paradigm reveals the tension, or contradiction, between the state as the primary vehicle for the pursuit of a narrowly or exclusively defined national interest, and the state as an effective and even necessary instrument for implementing a broader, normative, cosmopolitan agenda, in the form of a human rights regime for example, both domestically and internationally. Nonetheless, the human security paradigm does provide a way in which cosmopolitan attitudes towards war and peace can be translated into specific policies, in the form of the landmines treaty or limits on the production, availability and use of small arms and light weapons. In recent years the international community has also engaged in innovative but also controversial responses to new or post-modern wars, ostensibly to defend or to implement some of the values associated with the human security agenda, in the form of humanitarian intervention and peacebuilding. The cosmopolitan content of these two activities is assessed in the next two chapters.

## NOTES

1. Hampson, *Madness in the Multitude*, p. 6.
2. Ibid. p. 6.
3. McSweeney, *Security, Identity and Interests*, p. 33.
4. Ibid. p. 85.
5. See United Nations Development Programme (UNDP), *Human Development Report 1994*, pp. 24–30.
6. Ibid. p. 23.
7. Dunne and Wheeler, 'We the Peoples', p. 18.
8. Hampson, *Madness in the Multitude*, makes this point (p. 6), as does the Commission on Human Security, which says: 'The state continues to have the primary responsibility for security' (2003a).
9. King and Murray, 'Rethinking Human Security', p. 588.
10. Hampson, *Madness in the Multitude*, p. 37.
11. UNDP, *Human Development Report 1994*, p. 30.
12. Commission on Human Security, 'Outline of the Report of the Commission'.
13. Commission on Human Security, 'Press Release'.
14. Commission on Human Security, 'Plan for the Establishment of the Commission on Human Security'.
15. Commission on Human Security, 'Establishment of the Commission'.
16. Commission on Human Security, 'Plan for the Establishment of the Commission on Human Security'.
17. Hampson, *Madness in the Multitude*, p. 4.
18. Ibid. pp. 17–18.
19. Ibid. p. 33.

20. Ibid. p. 18.
21. Commission on Human Security, 'Outline of the Report of the Commission'.
22. UNDP, *Human Development Report 1994*, p. 32.
23. Dunne and Wheeler, 'We the Peoples', p. 18.
24. Ibid. p. 10.
25. Ibid. p. 18.
26. Ibid. p. 14.
27. Hampson, *Madness in the Multitude*, p. 23.
28. McRae, 'Human Security in a Globalized World', p. 20.
29. Hampson, *Madness in the Multitude*, p. 17.
30. Cited in Michael Small, 'Peacebuilding in Postconflict Societies', p. 75.
31. Hampson, *Madness in the Multitude*, p. 36.
32. Cf. ibid. Chapters 6 and 7.
33. Axworthy, 'Introduction', p. 9.
34. Golberg and Hubert, 'Case Study: The Security Council and the Protection of Civilians', p. 226.
35. Hampson, *Madness in the Multitude*, p. 34.
36. Ibid. p. 36.
37. Commission on Human Security, 'Outline of the Report of the Commission'.
38. Bajpai, 'The Idea of a Human Security Audit', p. 2.
39. Hampson, *Madness in the Multitude*, p. 45.
40. Commission on Human Security, 'Outline of the Report of the Commission'.
41. Robinson, 'Development and rights', p. 2.
42. UNDP, *Human Development Report 1994*, p. 24.
43. Hampson, *Madness in the Multitude*, p. 11.
44. McRae, 'Conclusion: International Relations and the New Diplomacy', p. 254.
45. Bajpai, 'The Idea of a Human Security Audit', p. 2.
46. Ibid. p. 2.
47. Dunne and Wheeler, 'We the Peoples', p. 10.
48. Bajpai, 'The Idea of a Human Security Audit', p. 1.
49. UNDP, *Human Development Report 1994*, p. 22.
50. Ibid. p. 24.
51. Ibid. p. 34.
52. Hampson, *Madness in the Multitude*, p. 15.
53. Commission on Human Security, 'Outline of the Report of the Commission'.
54. Hampson, *Madness in the Multitude*, p. 37.
55. McRae, 'Conclusion: International Relations and the New Diplomacy', p. 254.
56. Hampson, *Madness in the Multitude*, p. 53.
57. Ibid. pp. 53–60.
58. Ibid. p. 54.
59. McRae, 'Conclusion: International Relations and the New Diplomacy', p. 259.
60. Dunne and Wheeler, 'We the Peoples', p. 10.
61. Ibid. p. 19.
62. Ibid. p. 20.
63. Ibid. p. 21.
64. Ramcharan, 'Human rights and human security', p. 46.
65. Hataley and Nossal, 'The Limits of the Human Security Agenda', p. 7.

# CHAPTER 9

# HUMANITARIAN INTERVENTION, COSMOPOLITANISM AND PACIFISM

Over the last ten years or so, following the end of the Cold War, the issue of humanitarian intervention has become increasingly prominent in debates about the role of ethics in international affairs. Questions concerning the violation of state sovereignty and the use of armed force, in particular, have been central to debates about the morality of humanitarian intervention.

In ethical terms, humanitarian intervention involves a conflict between our cosmopolitan responsibility to protect and promote human rights because of their universality, and our obligation to respect state sovereignty as a crucial basis for international order and the possibility of moral and political community. Fulfilling one set of commitments can involve the violation of the other in situations where governments are actively abusing the fundamental rights of their own citizens, for example. Arguments critical of intervention can also be derived from concerns about the destructive consequences of any use of armed force, even for humanitarian purposes, in the form of human suffering and loss of life.

This chapter will examine these two ethical objections to international humanitarian intervention, that is, concerns about the violation of state sovereignty and the destructive impact of military action. It will then discuss three positions on the morality of humanitarian intervention, two of which provide positive responses to these objections, and one that remains critical.

Although the moral impetus for humanitarian intervention can be described as cosmopolitan, qualified arguments in favour of armed humanitarian intervention can be supported by some interpretations of international law, and also by applying at least some of the criteria of traditional just war theory. The chapter concludes with a pacifist or antimilitarist critique, which questions the humanitarian credentials of such interventions as well as their role in justifying and perpetuating the institutionalisation of military responses to political and social conflict. Thus, the issue of humanitarian intervention reveals a tension between the universal obligations implied by cosmopolitanism and antimilitarist or pacifist objections to the use of armed force, under situations of gross violations of human rights.

## I. JUSTIFYING HUMANITARIAN INTERVENTION

International humanitarian intervention is usually defined as the forceful infringement of a state's sovereignty in order to protect the fundamental human rights of those within its jurisdiction. In particular, Hubert and Bonser argue that the purpose of 'multilateral intervention in the affairs of a state must be to prevent or stop genocide or acute suffering and widespread loss of life, caused by massive and systematic violations of human rights'.[1] Such an infringement is often justified by claims that the state itself is involved in perpetrating such human rights abuses, is allowing them to occur or is unable to prevent them. Where a state is unable or unwilling to protect its own citizens, that responsibility shifts to the international community.[2] Thus, Knudsen defines humanitarian intervention as 'dictatorial or coercive interference in the sphere of jurisdiction of a sovereign state motivated or legitimated by humanitarian concerns'.[3] Furthermore, such intervention often involves the use of armed force.[4]

Thus, an important contrast between conventional UN peacekeeping operations and humanitarian intervention concerns the lack of consent of the states within whose jurisdiction the intervention occurs. 'Traditional peacekeeping missions pose little threat to norms of international sovereignty and territorial integrity because they serve with the consent of all parties and play a noncoercive role'.[5] Nonetheless, Hubert and Bonser emphasise that although humanitarian military intervention involves 'the use of non-consensual military means to fulfil humanitarian objectives', it 'is not undertaken against the integrity or political independence of any state or to seize territory'.[6]

According to proponents of humanitarian intervention, the increased emphasis on the universality and indivisibility of human rights places its own strong moral requirements on the international community. The protection, fulfilment and promotion of human rights involve cosmopolitan moral claims that transcend national or state boundaries precisely because of their supposed universality. It is this universality that provides a sort of moral or political legitimacy to the work of campaigning groups such as Amnesty International. Alex J. Bellamy, for example, argues that 'the contemporary international human rights regime' provides the normative basis for cosmopolitan advocates of humanitarian intervention.[7]

Furthermore, such universality implies that states have duties to all human beings, at least in the realm of fundamental rights, and not merely to their own citizens. Such duties come into conflict with the principle of national sovereignty, however, when states assert responsibility for protecting the fundamental rights of the citizens of other countries, even though their own governments either fulfil no such obligation or are actively violating these rights. In other words, 'extreme cases of human suffering' require a sort of cosmopolitan exemption from state sovereignty in the form of humanitarian intervention, according to this argument.[8] Proponents of 'cosmopolitan democracy', such as Daniele Archibugi, argue furthermore that humanitarian intervention should not be the responsibility of 'existing states' but rather of 'new institutions based on world citizenship. These institutions should be entitled to manage issues of global concern as well as to interfere within states whenever serious violations of human rights are committed.'[9]

While the protection of fundamental human rights may involve or require the violation of state sovereignty, the use of armed force may undermine, endanger or even violate fundamental human rights because of the destruction and human suffering it inevitably entails. The tensions between the universality of human rights and the principle of state sovereignty, and the protection of human rights and the use of armed force, lie at the core of debates about the ethics of humanitarian intervention.

## II. TWO ETHICAL OBJECTIONS TO HUMANITARIAN INTERVENTION

Conventional concerns with the protection of state sovereignty and the principle of nonintervention provide one important set of arguments against international humanitarian intervention. There are also those who oppose such intervention, not so much because it involves violations of state sovereignty, but because it involves the use of armed force. The concern here is that humanitarian intervention is merely a new justification for the militarism that pervades our societies and our political structures.

The principle of national sovereignty means that a state has supreme (or at least the highest degree of) authority over both its own territory and its own citizens. In terms of international relations, it implies that a state is not under the control of any other state, and has equal rights to other states within the international system. It involves, in other words, both formal equality between states and the principle of nonintervention in the internal affairs of another state.[10]

Recognition of state sovereignty, according to some critics of international humanitarian intervention, has been the foundation of attempts to impose and maintain order in relations between states in the international system. The principle of nonintervention, in particular, has been a cornerstone of international relations since the emergence of the nation-state as a basic political entity. Thus, as Knudsen points out, any 'right of humanitarian intervention represents a serious threat to the element of order constituted with international society'.[11]

China and Russia have consistently used their UN Security Council veto to block attempts to legitimate international humanitarian intervention on the grounds that it clearly violates the principles of state sovereignty and nonintervention. On the one hand, such use of the veto is a reaction to international concerns about their own domestic human rights records. As Chris Brown suggests: 'The doctrine of sovereignty can act to hide one form of oppression', internal repression, 'while bringing to the fore ... another', that is, external intervention or aggression.[12] On the other hand, as Nicholas Wheeler points out, there is a genuine concern that 'the doctrine of humanitarian intervention ... represents the West's assertion of a new "standard of civilization" that will be used to justify intervention against weaker states'. Such objections resonate with post-colonial states in particular, because for those countries still recovering from recent imperial domination the rhetoric of intervention may be humanitarian, but its implementation conveys echoes of a recent colonial past.[13] Humanitarian claims, for recently decolonised countries, can still mask a more sinister pursuit of great power interests.

A second moral question arises over the use of armed force or military action to implement such humanitarian intervention. One of the important ramifications of the principle of nonintervention is precisely that it places strict limits on the use of military force by any state, and armed humanitarian intervention appears to violate such limits. Furthermore, the destruction, human suffering and loss of life resulting from any military action can undermine the humanitarian objectives of armed intervention. I will return to this criticism towards the end of the chapter, since it forms the core of the antimilitarist or pacifist critique.

## III. THREE NORMATIVE RESPONSES TO ARMED HUMANITARIAN INTERVENTION

Those who support international humanitarian intervention as an emerging norm within existing international relations draw on both legal and moral arguments. In particular, they utilise aspects of international law as it has developed over the last fifty years, but also the moral criteria provided by traditional just war theory. This is not to suggest that either international law or just war theory necessarily imply support for international humanitarian intervention. Some critics of humanitarian intervention certainly draw on aspects of international law to bolster their arguments. The point is merely that some advocates of international humanitarian intervention find support for their positions within these legal or moral traditions.

## A. INTERNATIONAL LAW

International law provides responses to both objections to armed humanitarian intervention. In other words, the argument goes, if humanitarian intervention occurs in accordance with the requirements of international law, it will not threaten the basis of international order enshrined in the principles of state sovereignty and nonintervention. Furthermore, international law also provides explicit constraints on the use of armed force in international affairs, minimising its threat to humanitarian outcomes.

Legal scholars and governments often refer to the UN Charter as providing the standard principles governing the use of armed force under international law. The Charter contains both a general prohibition against the use of armed force (embodied in Article 2(4)), as well as the two exceptions to this prohibition. One exception concerns self-defence, or resistance against armed aggression, by member-states (Article 51). 'The other is when the use of force is authorized by the Security Council to maintain or restore international peace and security (Article 42).'[14]

In legal terms, according to Knudsen, 'the qualified right of humanitarian intervention' can be interpreted as an extension of the exception to the use of armed force embodied in Article 42.[15] In other words, situations of gross human rights abuses are viewed as a threat to international peace and security, and international humanitarian intervention is justified legally as a response to this threat. Furthermore, if the requirements of international peace and security (as exemplified by Article 42 of the UN Charter) are used to justify humanitarian intervention under international law, this implies not only that such intervention does not threaten the international order, it may even be necessary for its preservation.

Former UK Foreign Secretary Robin Cook has referred to 'internal strife' rather than 'international war' as 'the more common threat to peace and stability in today's world'.

> Yet the international law under which we still operate dates from the aftermath of the Second World War. It was drawn up to deal with the threat to international order of the time – aggressive invasion by a foreign power of another country. In response, it gave central importance to the sovereignty of governments and non-interference across borders.

He argues that international law must reflect the changing nature of such threats, in order to 'guide us on when to intervene to halt casualties within a nation which we would not tolerate between nations'.[16] In other words, the gross human rights abuses resulting from civil wars and internal armed conflicts must be seen to supplement territorial aggression as a threat to international peace and security, because of the nature of contemporary warfare. Chesterman claims, for example: 'The most basic transformation in the use of Security Council powers is that it now appears to be broadly accepted that a civil war or internal strife may constitute a threat to international peace and security.'[17]

Concerns about international peace and security and territorial aggression provide substantive constraints on the use of armed force in international affairs under international law. An important procedural constraint involves the need for UN Security Council authorisation, to prevent unilateral action and the abuse of such substantive principles for self-interested or hegemonic purposes. This procedural constraint or requirement has come under increasing challenge because of the constant threat (or safeguard) of the use of the veto by one or more of the permanent members of the Security Council to deprive an armed intervention of its legitimacy under international law.

This reflects the lack of agreement between governments and indeed the permanent members of the Security Council on the issue of humanitarian intervention. Some states continue to argue against any transgression of national sovereignty and the principle of nonintervention. On the other hand, some governments question the requirement that such interventions must be sanctioned by the UN Security Council, and must not be initiated unilaterally. This discussion has intensified since the NATO bombing campaign against Serbia in 1999, as revealed during the 'wide-ranging debate over the legitimacy and legality of humanitarian intervention' at the 54th General Assembly in September 1999.[18]

The so-called 'Bush doctrine' favouring not merely unilateral but also pre-emptive military action, enunciated in the aftermath of the Al Qaeda attacks of 11 September 2001, represents a further significant shift away from multilateralism and international law, enacted of course by means of the invasion and occupation of Iraq beginning in March 2003. Attempts to justify the case for war in Iraq in terms of positive international law, by means of either UN Security Council resolutions or self-defence, have been characterised as 'untenable'.[19]

Humanitarian intervention may be consistent with international law, providing it conforms to the requirements of the UN Charter. Furthermore, according to some of its proponents, while humanitarian intervention consistent with international law may contravene state sovereignty, it does not do so at the expense of international order, and may in fact be necessary to protect or preserve it.

Humanitarian intervention in accordance with the UN Charter must still satisfy the formidable procedural requirement of Security Council authorisation, however. Given the depth of disagreement between Security Council members over the legitimacy of humanitarian intervention, both as a matter of general principle and in specific instances, it seems that this requirement will be increasingly difficult to meet.

Unilateral humanitarian intervention, supported by arguments from popular sovereignty or the defence of fundamental human rights, may be one way of bypassing the practical impediment of UN Security Council authorisation. Both types of argument are derived more from normative political theory than from existing international law, however. It seems that arguments in favour of bypassing the procedural requirements of humanitarian intervention, in the form of UN Security Council authorisation, may have to be derived from more explicitly ethical, as distinct from legal, criteria.

## B. JUST WAR THEORY

Traditionally, just war theory has provided an obvious framework for addressing moral questions about the use of armed force in international affairs. Fixdal and Smith claim that: 'In Western culture, the Just War tradition is *the tradition* for addressing moral questions about when and how to use force.'[20] As discussed in Chapter 5, it could be argued that international humanitarian intervention presents the latest opportunity to rehabilitate this venerable approach to the ethics of war and military force.

Just war theory provides a set of criteria for assessing the morality of any war or military action. In other words, for any war or military action to be considered morally justified, it must satisfy these criteria. Furthermore, these criteria are conventionally divided into two basic categories, *jus ad bellum* and *jus in bello*, or criteria affecting the decision to go to war, and criteria concerning the conduct of war once it has been initiated.

In his recent book on humanitarian intervention, Nicholas Wheeler has drawn explicitly on just war theory to develop 'four requirements that an intervention must meet to qualify as humanitarian'. These are the requirements of just cause, last resort, proportionality and probability.[21] All four fall under the *jus ad bellum* category of just war criteria.

In modern times, the principle of self-defence against aggression has provided the substance of the just cause criterion. However, with the increased prevalence of internal armed conflicts over wars between states, we can see how concerns over the perpetration of gross human rights abuses within states might supplement the conventional emphasis on self-defence as the 'just cause' providing moral justification for the use of armed force. International humanitarian intervention to stop such abuses can then be supported as the fulfilment of the just cause criterion of just war theory. Thus, Wheeler defines a just cause as 'a supreme humanitarian emergency', which 'exists when the only hope of saving lives depends on outsiders coming to the rescue'.[22] Similarly, in his brief defence of unilateral humanitarian intervention in *Just and Unjust Wars*, Michael Walzer claims that: 'Against the enslavement or massacre of political opponents, national minorities, and religious sects, there may well be no help unless help comes from outside.'[23]

Hubert and Bonser also suggest the criterion of 'sustainability' for humanitarian intervention that can be perhaps connected to the requirement of just cause. In other words, the intervention must be 'part of a longer-term strategy to build and sustain peace'.[24]

In terms of the second criterion, the use of force must be a last resort, all other courses of action to stop massive violations of human rights, such as diplomacy, sanctions and other forms of international pressure, having been exhausted. The criterion of proportionality requires that the destruction and loss of lives resulting from armed humanitarian intervention be proportionate to (and certainly not exceed) the good that it is supposed to achieve (or at least the evil it is supposed to avert). Finally, according to Wheeler, 'there must be a high probability that the use of force will achieve a positive humanitarian outcome'.[25]

Wheeler considers these four to be minimum or 'threshold' requirements or criteria that every international humanitarian intervention must satisfy if it is to be justified morally. He only includes other traditional just war theory criteria, specifically 'humanitarian motives' (or 'right intention') and 'legality' (or sanction by a 'legitimate authority'), among four additional criteria that strengthen the 'humanitarian qualifications' of an intervention, without being morally necessary.[26]

Wheeler's analysis of the importance of 'right intention' to assessing humanitarian intervention is significant because the absence of such intention is central to some prominent critiques, which focus on the self-interested or hegemonic motives behind interventions putatively aimed at protecting human rights. Chomsky, for example, refers to the claim that 'the right of humanitarian intervention, if it exists, is premised on the good faith of those intervening' as a 'truism'.[27]

Wheeler, on the other hand, suggests that the problem with emphasising humanitarian motives as a requirement for legitimate humanitarian intervention 'is that it takes the intervening state as the referent object for analysis rather than the victims who are rescued as a consequence of the use of force'. In other words, from the point of view of the victims of human rights abuses, what counts is success in ending or preventing these abuses, rather than the motives of the intervening state. Motives are relevant only insofar as they influence or affect humanitarian outcomes, in accordance with the 'probability' criterion.[28] Motives can be understood, in this sense, as the expression of desired outcomes. As such, they are only one factor affecting the likelihood of achieving these outcomes.

The UN Security Council is the 'legitimate authority' for the contemporary use of armed force in international affairs, in the sense that 'the Security Council has the legal authority under the Chapter VII provisions of the Charter to authorise military enforcement action'. We have already seen the practical difficulties associated with obtaining Security Council authorisation for humanitarian intervention, however, because of the use of the veto by its permanent members. This, combined with problems associated with possible sources of the legality of unilateral humanitarian intervention, in the absence of Security Council authorisation, removes 'legality' as one of Wheeler's threshold requirements for the legitimacy of a humanitarian intervention.[29]

One implication of this approach is that the four threshold criteria can be used to circumvent the requirements of international law (particularly the prohibition against unilateral action) without undermining the moral legitimacy of an intervention.[30] The need to respond to a supreme humanitarian emergency, in accordance with the 'just cause' criterion, can override the requirement of Security Council authorisation, for example.[31]

While this may weaken the appeal to international law as a basis for humanitarian intervention, it can help overcome the paralysis induced by the need for Security Council authorisation. Furthermore, according to Wheeler, this can be done without undermining 'the pillars of interstate order', so long as the four threshold criteria are adhered to consistently. In other words, even unilateral humanitarian intervention will not jeopardise the international order so long as moral criteria are substituted for international law in determining its legitimacy.[32]

The danger with this sort of argument, as Wheeler recognises, is that it implies a 'conflict between legality and morality' that 'weakens international law'.[33] Humanitarian intervention becomes the international equivalent of civil disobedience by states, according to which the law is deliberately broken in the name of higher standards of justice or morality.

This suggests that just war criteria should be used as the basis for changing or modifying international law, rather than overriding or superseding it. Perhaps the 'legitimate authority' of the Security Council concerning humanitarian intervention needs to be supplemented explicitly by other sources of legality governing unilateral intervention, in the form of customary international law reflecting both state practice and *opinio juris*, or beliefs about the legality of that practice. Although this presents the proponents of humanitarian intervention with an enormous practical challenge, it seems to be the only way they can promote the ethical requirements associated with just war theory without simultaneously undermining the already precarious jurisdiction of international law over the protection of human rights and the use of armed force.

One of Wheeler's threshold requirements, proportionality, suggests another area of difficulty concerning just war criteria as a source of legitimacy for humanitarian intervention. The criterion of proportionality explicitly addresses the destructive consequences of military action, even when initiated or engaged in for humanitarian purposes. These consequences form the basis of the pacifist or antimilitarist critique of humanitarian intervention.

## C. PACIFISM

Those who argue against humanitarian intervention as a subversion of the foundations of international order are particularly concerned to defend the principle or norm of national sovereignty, with its concomitant doctrine of nonintervention in the internal affairs of states. There are also those who object to humanitarian intervention not so much as an attack on national sovereignty, but because they are suspicious of the use of armed force under any circumstances. They are particularly concerned with the destruction, human suffering and loss of life resulting from any military action, for whatever reason.

Thus, the notion of a 'humanitarian war' or armed humanitarian intervention becomes a 'tragic contradiction'.[34] The resort to armed force results almost inevitably in nonhumanitarian outcomes. Wheeler states, for example, that during the UN-sanctioned 'Operation Restore Hope' in Somalia: 'It is estimated that 6–8,000 Somali citizens were killed as the US employed force indiscriminately.'[35] Similarly, Chesterman cites one US military operation (the 'Olympic Hotel battle') in which: 'At least 500 and as many as 1,000 Somalis – many of them civilians – were killed in the firefight.'[36]

Knudsen identifies such outcomes as an 'operational problem' associated with armed humanitarian intervention, that is, that there is always 'the possibility that intervention will do more harm than good to the suffering civilians',[37] as in this example from Somalia. As an 'operational problem', however, the implication is that such a possibility or danger can be avoided if humanitarian interventions are implemented or engaged in correctly. Thus, Knudsen distinguishes such operational problems from 'the systemic problems of humanitarian intervention' (which include its putative threat to the international order).[38]

Characterising the nonhumanitarian consequences of humanitarian intervention as an operational problem suggests that perhaps we could learn from the example of Somalia in order to prevent large numbers of civilian casualties resulting from other instances of military action to achieve humanitarian objectives. Somalia, after all, is a relatively early example of humanitarian intervention under the 'New World Order'. Later that same decade, however, NATO's bombing campaign against Serbia did not provide much evidence that such 'operational' problems are being corrected. NATO seemed more concerned about minimising its own military casualties than reducing the risk to the civilian population it claimed to be protecting.

> Given the low risks run by NATO air-crews, and the failure of the air campaign to stop the ethnic cleansing by Serb army and police forces, the unsettling conclusion can be drawn that NATO's desire to undertake a 'casualty-free' intervention was achieved at the expense of inflicting great suffering on Kosovar Albanians and Serb civilians.[39]

Similarly, Hoffman claims that: 'In the case of Kosovo, the immediate effect of the bombing operation was the massive expulsion of the Kosovars whose protection was the objective of the war, and the US preference for the immunity of their combatants increased casualties among noncombatants, both Serbs and Kosovars.'[40] And according to Hampson, NATO itself acknowledged that 'the numbers of Kosovar refugees more than doubled during the air campaign', so that ultimately 90 per cent of the population had been displaced either internally or externally.[41] The loss of life and human suffering by civilian populations resulting from military action, even for humanitarian purposes, may turn out to be a much more intractable problem than is indicated by Knudsen's 'operational' description.

The examples of Somalia and Kosovo illustrate a concern that the proportionality criterion of just war theory will not be satisfied by the use of military force, even for humanitarian objectives. This involves a quasi-utilitarian assessment of anticipated outcomes, of destructive consequences versus benefits attained. There always remains the empirical possibility, however, that some humanitarian interventions may satisfy the proportionality criterion, even if this possibility remains remote from an antimilitarist perspective.

As discussed in Chapter 6, the antiwar principles of pacifists sometimes transcend the utilitarian calculations implied by the proportionality criterion, however. Rather, they embody a more fundamental non-consequentialist commitment to the value of human life that goes beyond such utilitarian considerations. In other words, prohibitions against the taking of human life, for whatever reason, supersede (or 'trump') other kinds of ethical considerations, including the projected outcomes of armed humanitarian intervention. The value of human life is such that it cannot be subjected to the utilitarian calculus.

One difficulty with this critique of humanitarian intervention is that it emphasises our obligation to respect the fundamental rights of other human beings (including the rights to life and personal security) at the expense of our equal duty to protect those rights, where we are in a position to do so. Terry Nardin, for example, refers to 'humanitarian intervention as an expression of the basic moral duty to protect the innocent from violence'.[42] In other words, under certain conditions efforts to protect the fundamental human rights of a section of a civilian population may justifiably involve placing the lives or personal security of some noncombatants at risk.

If we accept an equal obligation to both respect and protect fundamental human rights, where it is in our power to do so, then an absolute objection to the taking of human life under any circumstances (whether deliberately or not) may be replaced by only marginally less stringent moral conditions involving a combination of just war criteria. Placing civilian lives at risk in the context of humanitarian intervention may only be justified providing noncombatants are not deliberately targeted (the principle of discrimination), all efforts have been made to avoid noncombatant casualties (last resort and 'due care'), and the level of risk to civilians is proportionate to the probability of achieving humanitarian outcomes. Similarly, Terry Nardin argues that 'above all, those who intervene must respect the moral laws that forbid harming innocent people as a means to an end and that require a fair distribution of risk (by prescribing attention to considerations of 'proportionality' and 'due care') between the intervening forces and those they aim to assist'.[43]

The amplification of the just war principle of discrimination by due care as a *jus in bello* criterion in the context of armed humanitarian intervention implies that it is not sufficient merely to avoid deliberately targeting noncombatants. We must employ instead the much stricter requirement that all efforts must be made to minimise civilian casualties, or that the lives of noncombatants can only be placed at risk as a last resort, in accordance with the principle of 'due care'.

Thus, while NATO's bombing campaign may have satisfied the principle of discrimination, in the sense that no civilians were deliberately targeted, it most certainly did not satisfy this more stringent condition. It could be argued, furthermore, that NATO's use of a high-level bombing campaign diminished its capacity to prevent the ethnic cleansing of Kosovar Albanians by Serb forces on the ground, thus reducing any probability of achieving immediate humanitarian outcomes while at the same time increasing the risk to the civilian population.

An a priori or nonconsequentialist pacifist objection to the taking of human life under any circumstances may not be supported by cosmopolitan arguments from human rights. While it is true that arguments for human rights can be developed from both consequentialist and non-consequentialist (or deontological) normative theories, the crucial tension remains between the pacifist prohibition against the taking of human life under any circumstances and a cosmopolitan requirement to protect as well as respect human life in accordance with fundamental human rights.

Even so, the use of armed force to protect human rights can only be justified under conditions that also facilitate full respect for those rights through minimising the risks to noncombatants. Such conditions require a much more stringent interpretation of the traditional *jus in bello* criterion of discrimination that goes further than merely prohibiting the deliberate targeting of civilians. It should be noted, however, that this tightening of *jus in bello* requirements as applied to armed humanitarian intervention may only mollify pacifist concerns about their nonhumanitarian outcomes for civilian populations. It will not satisfy pacifist objections to the taking of any human life, including the lives of enemy combatants or of those perpetrating aggression or human rights abuses against a civilian population.

Both consequentialist and nonconsequentialist (or deontological) pacifist or antimilitarist objections to armed humanitarian intervention are derived from what they claim to be its immediate, almost inevitable, non-humanitarian outcomes. In addition, there is a concern about its longer-term structural or institutional consequences. In other words, the pacifist or antimilitarist critics of armed humanitarian intervention are concerned that such interventions will perpetuate the ideology of militarism and the institutionalisation of military responses to conflict that permeate our political, social and economic structures through processes of militarisation.[44]

> Militarization ... suggests more than the strengthening of militaristic institutions directly engaged in political conflicts. It also means the social acceptance of militarism as the legitimate and correct form of political practice in cases of crisis.[45]

Armed humanitarian intervention, in other words, merely reinforces the social and political processes that give rise to the problems it is meant to address.

The real challenge, according to Kofi Annan, is to protect human rights through developing a culture of nonviolent preventative diplomacy.[46] The danger is that the renewed emphasis on military responses to conflict epitomised by the doctrine of armed humanitarian intervention will preclude such nonviolent, or at least nonmilitary, approaches to dealing with conflict, and may in fact entrench the cycles of confrontation and violence that give rise to it. As Wheeler says: 'The literature on humanitarian intervention tends to focus on the use of force, but by the time this type of intervention is contemplated, many opportunities for preventative action have been missed.'[47]

One difficulty with this sort of criticism is that it tends to be counter-factual. Specific examples or credible suggestions of effective nonmilitary or nonviolent responses to large-scale abuses of human rights in the context of armed conflict (like those that occurred in Rwanda, Kosovo, East Timor or western Sudan) need to be provided for it to be fully convincing. If this were done, we could then combine it with the human rights-based argument to produce the essential antimilitarist critique of armed humanitarian intervention, that it unnecessarily jeopardises civilian lives and personal security because there are other less destructive, nonviolent responses available.

The critique of humanitarian intervention as a violation of national sovereignty, and thus as an attack on one of the fundamental principles of international order, can be overcome conceivably by the appropriate application of emerging norms embodied both by international law and particular moral criteria derived from just war theory. There are practical limitations to the use of existing international law as a sanction or justification for humanitarian intervention, however, resulting from the threat or use of the veto in the UN Security Council. This may be ameliorated by the use of just war criteria to allow more unilateral forms of military action for humanitarian reasons, but only if these can be credibly integrated into international law.

The pacifist or antimilitarist view of armed humanitarian intervention as a self-contradictory principle or doctrine remains an issue, however. In other words, according to this critique, the use of armed force is not consistent with obtaining humanitarian objectives, as illustrated by the UN intervention in Somalia and the NATO bombing campaign against Serbia. The loss of life and human suffering resulting from military action cannot be reconciled with intervention for supposedly humanitarian reasons. Furthermore, armed intervention merely perpetuates the institutionalisation of military responses to political and social conflict, and the ideology of militarism used to justify such responses.

What we require are effective peaceful or nonviolent alternatives to armed intervention that can satisfy our cosmopolitan responsibility to both respect and protect fundamental human rights. Peacebuilding and conflict prevention as forms of international conflict management represent post-Cold War attempts by the international community to implement such strategies.

# NOTES

1. Hubert and Bonser, 'Humanitarian Military Intervention', p. 114.
2. See the Report of the International Commission on Intervention and State Sovereignty, *The Responsibility to Protect*, for example.
3. Knudsen, 'Humanitarian Intervention Revisited', p. 146.
4. Oudraat identifies the use of armed force and economic sanctions as 'the two main coercive instruments' available to states when considering intervention. De Jonge Oudraat, 'Humanitarian Intervention', p. 427.
5. Ottaway and Lacina, 'International Interventions and Imperialism', p. 76.
6. Hubert and Bonser, 'Humanitarian Military Intervention', pp. 111, 114.
7. Bellamy, 'Ethics and Intervention', p. 138.
8. Ibid. p. 138.
9. Archibugi, 'Principles of Cosmopolitan Democracy', p. 216.
10. Knudsen, 'Humanitarian Intervention Revisited', p. 150.
11. Ibid. p. 150.
12. Brown, *International Relations Theory*, p. 131.
13. Wheeler, 'Humanitarian Intervention after Kosovo', p.118.
14. Oudraat, 'Humanitarian Intervention', p. 421. See also Chesterman, *Just War or Just Peace?*, p. 1.
15. Knudsen, 'Humanitarian Intervention Revisited', p. 156.
16. Cook, 'Guiding Humanitarian Intervention'.
17. Chesterman, *Just War or Just Peace?*, p. 129.
18. Wheeler, *Saving Strangers*, p. 285.
19. Bellamy, 'Ethics and Intervention', pp. 134–6.
20. Fixdal and Smith, 'Humanitarian Intervention and Just War', p. 285.
21. Wheeler, *Saving Strangers*, pp. 33–4.
22. Ibid. p. 34.
23. Walzer, *Just and Unjust Wars*, p. 101.
24. Hubert and Bonser, 'Humanitarian Military Intervention', p. 119.
25. Wheeler, *Saving Strangers*, p. 34.
26. Ibid. p.52.
27. Chomsky, *The New Military Humanism*, p. 74.
28. Wheeler, *Saving Strangers*, p. 38.
29. Ibid. p. 41ff.
30. See also Walzer's discussion of unilateral humanitarian intervention, *Just and Unjust Wars*, pp. 107–8.
31. Wheeler, *Saving Strangers*, p. 41.
32. Ibid. p. 295.
33. Ibid. p. 41.
34. Ibid. p. 35.
35. Wheeler, 'Humanitarian Intervention after Kosovo', p. 116.
36. Chesterman, *Just War or Just Peace?*, p. 143.
37. Knudsen, 'Humanitarian Intervention Revisited', p. 152.
38. Ibid. p. 151.
39. Wheeler, 'Humanitarian Intervention after Kosovo', p. 127.
40. Hoffman, 'The Debate about Intervention', p. 279.
41. Hampson, *Madness in the Multitude*, p. 143.
42. Nardin, 'The Moral Basis of Humanitarian Intervention', p. 70. He also suggests: 'If humanitarian intervention means acting to protect human rights, there are many such

rights besides the right to life that might be threatened, including rights against torture, arbitrary detention, and racial discrimination. But usually only the gravest violations, like genocide and ethnic cleansing, are held to justify armed intervention', p. 66.

43. Nardin, 'The Moral Basis of Humanitarian Intervention', p. 69.
44. See Krippendorff, 'The state and militarism after 11 September', pp. 14–15.
45. Uyangoda, 'Militarization, Violent State, Violent Society', p. 124.
46. Wheeler, *Saving Strangers*, p. 302.
47. Ibid. p. 123.

# CHAPTER 10

# PEACEBUILDING AND INTERNATIONAL CONFLICT MANAGEMENT

The central aim of peacebuilding is to provide those countries emerging out of armed conflicts with the skills and resources they require not only to rebuild but also to prevent the recurrence of political violence. Thus, effective peacebuilding requires an understanding of the dynamics of social and political conflict as well as innovative nonviolent responses to it.

Despite the relative success of post-settlement peacebuilding under UN auspices in Mozambique (and, more recently, East Timor), its current prospects are perhaps much less hopeful or promising. The main challenge to peacebuilding as a form of 'conflict management' in the context of the current international situation is the resurrection of war as a deliberate instrument of foreign policy (in the form of the Bush doctrine and 'pre-emptive strikes') combined with the threat this poses to multilateralism, represented primarily by the UN. The type of involvement, or lack of involvement, of the international community in post-Taliban Afghanistan provides a stark contrast to the role of ONUMOZ and the UN in Mozambique, for example.

At a deeper level, some critics challenge the notion that peacebuilding is merely a form of international conflict management. Peacebuilding can be a mechanism for transmitting Western values and institutions from the so-called developed world to so-called developing or emerging countries, or from the core to the periphery. Peacebuilding must be rooted in cosmopolitan values, and not only the multilateral institutions associated with internationalism, in order to ensure it does not become just another vehicle for great power hegemony.

In particular, peacebuilding involves the transmission of the Westphalian model of the state to countries emerging from civil war or internal armed conflict. Attempts to establish such states may play an ambiguous role concerning the violence-prevention component of peacebuilding in the context of so-called 'new' or 'post-modern' wars, however, since the formation, control and legitimacy of the state is so often precisely what is in dispute in such wars.

141

## I. PEACEBUILDING IN THE POST-COLD WAR ERA

Peacebuilding emerged as a popular concept through *An Agenda for Peace* in the early 1990s (1992), in the optimism of the immediate post-Cold War period and George Bush Senior's 'New World Order', although Johan Galtung was already using the term some decades previously. *An Agenda for Peace* was 'released after the Security Council met in January 1992 – at the level of heads of government for the first time in its history – to discuss the UN agenda in the post-Cold War world'.[1] Both Galtung and Boutros Boutros-Ghali discuss peacebuilding in connection with the related concepts and activities of peacemaking and peacekeeping.[2]

Boutros-Ghali referred to peacemaking as 'action to bring hostile parties to agreement, essentially through ... peaceful means'.[3] This can include various forms of mediation, negotiation and conflict resolution as well as more conventional forms of diplomacy.

So-called 'classic peacekeeping', conventionally associated with UN intervention in armed conflicts (pre-1990), involves the impartial imposition of the armed forces of uninvolved countries between warring or conflicting groups in order to preserve or protect whatever peace agreements or political settlements these groups have been able to achieve. Traditional peacekeeping missions are established under the auspices of Chapter VI of the UN Charter, 'at the invitation of the states where they will be deployed, to support a peace agreement previously reached by the warring parties'. Ottaway and Lacina refer to them as 'essentially a confidence-building measure; each party to the conflict can rely on UN personnel to assess the other side's compliance with the peace agreement and thus feels more secure in honouring its own commitment'.[4] Peacekeeping has also come to include the implementation of the immediate terms of such agreements under UN auspices, as in the case of ONUMOZ in Mozambique.

Peacebuilding, as the final phase or stage of these three basic components of a peace process, involves a combination of post-settlement reconstruction and violence prevention. Thus, Boutros-Ghali defines peacebuilding as 'action to identify and support structures which will tend to strengthen and solidify peace in order to avoid a relapse into conflict'.[5] As we shall see, the post-conflict peacebuilding activities of the UN have tended to focus on 'the newer task of state reconstruction', in addition to 'the classic task of supervising and monitoring the implementation of peace agreements'.[6]

In other words, there is an assumption that all armed conflicts, no matter how protracted and apparently intractable, are both finite and resolvable through these processes of 'international conflict management'.

As George Mitchell said in an address to the Royal Irish Academy in November 2002, 'there is no such thing as a conflict that cannot be ended – peace can ultimately prevail'. Conflicts are created by human beings and they can also be ended by human beings. There is also an assumption that armed conflict is not merely resolvable, but also preventable, and that 'conflict management' can somehow replace or displace war and armed force as responses to political and social conflict.

It was thought that, in the aftermath of the Cold War, protracted local or regional conflict in, for example, Central America (El Salvador, Guatemala) and southern Africa (Mozambique, South Africa) could also be resolved. To some extent, this optimism was justified, with peace processes becoming entrenched and ending armed conflict in many of these regions or countries.

There were also numerous new, at least equally bitter and destructive conflicts in the 1990s however, such as Somalia, Rwanda, ex-Yugoslavia, Chechnya, West Africa and the Democratic Republic of Congo, that perhaps represent failures or at least limits to this form of 'international conflict management'. These are perhaps examples of what Mary Kaldor and others have referred to as 'new wars' or 'post-modern wars', because they are largely internal or 'intra-state' and because nonstate actors play such a prominent role in them.[7]

## II. SOME BASIC CHARACTERISTICS OF PEACEBUILDING

Table 10.1 summarises some suggested characteristics of peacebuilding, organised thematically. The main distinctions concern the international and domestic, and so-called 'negative peace' and 'positive peace' components of peacebuilding.

The international dimension of peacebuilding is both institutional and normative. The institutional element stresses peacebuilding as a multilateral activity, with a strong role for the UN in particular. Kofi Annan, for his part, has reiterated the importance of peacebuilding and conflict prevention as central activities and responsibilities of the United Nations. In his June 2001 report on 'The prevention of armed conflict', for example, he states 'conflict prevention lies at the heart of the mandate of the United Nations in the maintenance of international peace and security'.[8]

The normative element concerns the underlying values both implicit and explicit in peacebuilding, including a commitment to human rights, economic and social development, and processes of democratisation. Furthermore, these values or norms are supposed to be universally relevant and applicable, and connect peacebuilding to a broadly cosmopolitan agenda. Mary Kaldor suggests that peacebuilding requires 'an alliance between international organizations and local advocates of cosmopolitanism' in response to 'new wars', precisely because these wars involve a contest over state legitimacy and the disintegration of social and political repositories of shared values or norms.[9]

I have suggested that the domestic dimension of peacebuilding can be divided, at least for analytical purposes, into 'positive peace' and 'negative peace' elements, a distinction that Galtung utilised in his seminal article 'Violence, Peace and Peace Research'.[10] Broadly speaking, 'positive peace' refers to the elimination or alleviation of the underlying causes of war and armed conflict through initiating processes of peaceful social, economic and political change. As Boutros-Ghali suggests in *An Agenda for Peace*, 'the deepest causes of conflict include economic despair, social injustice, and political oppression'.[11]

'Negative peace' refers to the cessation of what Galtung refers to as 'direct' or physical violence. It is in this sense that peace becomes the opposite, or the absence, of war or armed conflict.

'Positive peace' is also linked to broader conceptions of justice, both procedural and distributive, as providing the essential conditions for a peaceful society and preventing the recurrence of armed conflict. 'Negative peace', on the other hand, can be connected to security, or the removal of immediate threats to one's wellbeing and survival, bringing together these two elements, justice and security, of what we might mean by 'peace' more generally.

Peacebuilding is also concerned with building or developing institutions and procedures for dealing with conflicts nonviolently, or what Oliver Ramsbotham refers to as 'confronting the challenge of "Clausewitz in reverse"', so 'that post-war politics is a continuation of the conflict albeit transmuted into non-military mode'.[12] The aim of peacebuilding is not to end conflict, which is inevitable and can be a creative force for change in societies, but rather to ensure that such conflicts can be dealt with without resorting to destructive physical violence.

As Charles Lerche suggests:

> conflict among groups is really politics as usual, but when it takes an overtly violent form it indicates the political system can no longer contain this inevitable competition for material and non-material stakes. We should not, therefore, expect relations between any politically significant cleavage groups to be definitively transformed into a state of harmony.[13]

Instead, they need to acquire the capacity and the institutions to deal with conflict nonviolently, so that peacebuilding 'should include the search for a model of governance and social relations that enables all groups in society to deal equitably and creatively with conflict'.[14]

*Table 10.1:* Some basic characteristics of peacebuilding

Adapted from *An Agenda for Peace*:

- Post-settlement reconstruction
- Aimed at violence prevention

At the international level:

- Multilateral, that is, under the auspices of multilateral organisations, especially the UN
- Reflecting a concern with international norms (sometimes embodied in international law), that is, human rights, development

At the domestic level ('positive peace'/justice):

- Involving or strengthening civil society (for example, NGOs, GROs,[a] churches, trade unions), partly as a way of legitimising or gaining acceptance for peace agreements or peace processes [social]
- Democratisation, state-building, good governance (that is, transparent, accountable, not corrupt), rule of law [political]
- Economic development, poverty eradication, overcoming inequality [economic]

At the domestic level ('negative peace'/security):

- Demobilisation of combatants
- Disarmament through the 'decommissioning' or elimination of weapons
- Demilitarisation both institutionally (for example, through reform of the security forces) and also ideologically (peace education, and so on)

---

[a] NGOs refers to nongovernmental organisations generally, GROs refers to 'grass-roots' or community-based organisations.

This concern with peacebuilding as a form of conflict resolution or conflict transformation capacity-building is reflected in the recent definition provided by the Canadian Peacebuilding Coordinating Committee (CPCC).

> Peacebuilding is the effort to strengthen the prospects for internal peace and decrease the likelihood of violent conflict. The overarching goal of peacebuilding is to enhance the indigenous capacity of a society to manage conflict without violence.[15]

While the international community can play a vital role in an imme-diate post-war situation, the ultimate objective of peacebuilding must be to develop or create or activate domestic or indigenous capacities for dealing with conflict nonviolently.

Thus, we can say that the 'peace' sought through post-settlement peacebuilding activities consists of three core elements or values: justice (distributive and procedural), security and nonviolence. The first two concern desired outcomes of peacebuilding (positive and negative peace), while the third involves the methods by which these are to be achieved and sustained, reflected through a commitment to developing or utilising indigenous capacities for conflict resolution.

The CPCC has also produced a 'Peacebuilding Activities Chart' that provides an 'operational definition' of peacebuilding divided into eleven categories, illustrating what the concept means in practice. This chart was produced as a result of a 1997 census of Canadian NGO peacebuilding activities, and complements the more analytical definition provided in Table 10.1.[16] Catholic Relief Services has also produced a similar 'opera-tional definition' of peacebuilding, based on their own field experience, in the form of 'sixteen categories of peacebuilding activities'.[17]

David Last and Oliver Ramsbotham have each provided detailed analytical definitions of peacebuilding in schematic form, which coincide more or less with the different aspects of the domestic dimension of peacebuilding outlined in Table 10.1. Last bases his analysis of peace-building requirements on the core peacebuilding tasks identified by the CPCC. Both Last and Ramsbotham also refer to another, psychological, dimension of peacebuilding, concerned with 'healing psychological wounds' (Ramsbotham) or 'psycho-social trauma' (Last), which they link to processes of reconciliation.[18]

Gender is of course an important cross-cutting theme affecting all aspects of peacebuilding. It has been suggested that conflict affects men and women differently precisely because of the different social roles assigned to them and relations of power between them. Thus, the 'Gender and Peacebuilding' workshop at the recent International Conference Towards Better Peace Building Practice suggested: 'As gender is embedded in relations of power/powerlessness it is important that when under-standing violent conflict it is viewed from a gender perspective.'[19] And Lerche claims that it is 'well documented that women, who do much of the essential work and domestic production in society, are most affected by widespread conflict'.[20]

Such gender relations can also permeate efforts to emerge from and overcome violent conflict through peacebuilding. 'The conventional wisdom is that men negotiate the peace while women build it.'[21] Elisabeth

Porter suggests that while women are central to informal peace processes and community peacebuilding, they continue to be excluded from formal peace negotiations and related political procedures.[22] These are merely some of the conventional gender roles that may need to be challenged by peacebuilding activities genuinely concerned with a commitment to a positive peace, or justice, component. Thus, Porter argues 'women's inclusion in all stages of peace processes is crucial for inclusive social justice'.[23] The gender dimension of peacebuilding has been recognised by both the European Parliament and the UN Security Council (Resolution 1325 on Women, Peace and Security).[24]

## III. PEACEKEEPING AND PEACEBUILDING IN MOZAMBIQUE

The United Nations Operation in Mozambique (ONUMOZ) has been credited with 'one of the most successful transitions from war to peace in recent times'.[25] ONUMOZ is an example of 'second generation' peace-keeping, with perhaps more in common with post-settlement peacebuild-ing, or active efforts to secure a sustainable peace, than with 'classic' or 'first generation' peacekeeping.

The sixteen-year civil war in Mozambique (1977–92) is an example of a post-colonial 'state control' conflict in a Cold War context, facilitated by the intervention of outside powers. Mozambique became independent of Portuguese rule in 1975. This was followed by the prolonged and vicious civil war between Frelimo (Mozambique Liberation Front) and Renamo (Mozambique National Resistance) over control of the country. Frelimo had led the armed struggle against the Portuguese, setting up a one-party state after their withdrawal. Renamo was established with the sponsorship of Rhodesia in 1977, which was subsequently assumed by apartheid South Africa in 1980.

External interests were in many ways responsible for sustaining and intensifying the civil war between Frelimo and Renamo for control of Mozambique. Both Rhodesia and South Africa provided crucial military and logistical support for Renamo. Similarly, the Frelimo government received vital military support from Zimbabwe and Tanzania. Cold War politics also undoubtedly played a role because of Frelimo's openly Marxist-Leninist rhetoric and policies for the first ten years or so of independence. The Frelimo government received essential political and military support from the Soviet Union and Eastern European countries during this time.

When these external forces began to lose interest in Mozambique, in the context of the end of the Cold War and of apartheid in South Africa, the result was a military stalemate. Both sides realised they were not in a position to defeat their opponent militarily. The Frelimo government explained that the country 'was suffering badly from the effects of the cessation of aid from the former USSR and the Eastern European countries'. Direct negotiations between Renamo and Frelimo began in 1990, resulting ultimately in the General Peace Agreement of 1992. The civil war had produced over one million deaths and five million refugees, affecting directly approximately one-third of the total population.[26]

The role of ONUMOZ was to facilitate the implementation of the General Peace Agreement. It operated within a finite and relatively short period of time, between the signing of the Agreement and the national election in December 1994.

According to Aldo Ajello, the UN Secretary-General's special representative in charge of ONUMOZ, the operation had four basic components: political, military, humanitarian and electoral.[27] The key element of the political component was the Supervision and Monitoring Commission (CSC), which replaced the government in all matters related to the implementation of the General Peace Agreement. The members of the CSC were the two main political parties (Frelimo and Renamo) and various international partners, and it was chaired by the UN.

The military component consisted of both UN observers, responsible for monitoring the demobilisation process, for example, and five infantry battalions, protecting the delivery of humanitarian aid and the return of refugees and displaced people. The humanitarian component was coordinated by the United Nations Office of the Humanitarian Assistance Coordinator (UNOHAC). Its 'mandate was to coordinate the humanitarian assistance of the UN organizations and, to the extent possible, of nongovernmental organizations (NGOs)' to displaced people and returning refugees, for example.[28]

'The electoral component was relatively small. Its mandate was simply to monitor and observe.' Organizing the elections was the responsibility of the National Election Commission.[29] The election returned Frelimo to power, this time with a democratic mandate. A key factor in the success of the peace process was Renamo's acceptance of the election results, and its continued commitment to pursuing its objectives by peaceful political means, exemplifying the process of 'Clausewitz in reverse'. Perhaps the greatest achievement of ONUMOZ was the demobilisation and reintegration of eighty thousand combatants from both sides of the civil war.

A key reason for this success was financial, in the form of the Reintegration Support Scheme (RSS). The RSS was an 'ad hoc Trust Fund' provided by the international donor community and administered by the UNDP, which provided eighteen months' wages to each soldier in

*Table 10.2:* Eight lessons from the Mozambican experience[a]

---

1. A strong will for peace on the part of all the parties involved in the conflict is an essential prerequisite for the success of a peacekeeping operation.
2. A solid peace agreement provides the essential basis for a successful peacekeeping operation.
3. A strong political structure should be established to manage the peace process.
4. The United Nations should be given an active political role in this structure as the engine of the process and not a passive role as an observer.
5. The international community should be an active player in the peace process.
6. The presentation and consolidation of peace should be the top priority in a peacekeeping operation.
7. Rules and procedures should be applied with the required flexibility.
8. The special representative of the secretary-general must be carefully selected.

---

[a] Ajello, 'Mozambique: Implementation of the 1992 Peace Agreement', pp. 640–1.

addition to the six months' wages provided by the government under the terms of the General Peace Agreement.

According to Ajello, the RSS achieved two or perhaps three important results. 'It prevented violence and banditry and hence helped to establish a peaceful environment in which the electoral campaign could take place.' Furthermore, it avoided what he referred to as the 'Angola scenario', in which both sides were able to hold on to 'a reserve of troops … as a safety net'. It 'also had the side effect of reducing the number of soldiers interested in joining the new army'.[30]

Thus, ONUMOZ was successful in terms of the 'negative peace' objectives of peacebuilding in Mozambique, through bringing a definitive end to the civil war and achieving the demobilisation and reintegration of combatants. In terms of 'positive peace' objectives, armed conflict has been replaced by political competition in the context of formal democratic structures, such as a federal parliament and regular elections. Economically, Mozambique has achieved high rates of growth but remains heavily dependent on foreign aid and constrained by debt and World Bank/IMF (International Monetary Fund) conditionalities.

A vital ingredient of this 'positive peace' component of peacebuilding in Mozambique was Frelimo's prior forced conversion from state socialism to liberal market democracy. The Frelimo government accepted this as a condition of World Bank/IMF loans because of its desperate need for funds as a result of the destruction of the physical and social infrastructure of the country during the civil war.[31] 'The peacebuilding mission, in other words, reinforced and expedited a process of political and economic liberalisation which had been ongoing since the early 1980s.'[32]

Ajello has suggested eight lessons 'from the Mozambican experience', which are summarised in Table 10.2. These emphasise the importance of a strong commitment to the process on the part of all groups involved in the conflict, as well as the importance of the international community more generally and the UN in particular.

## IV. CHALLENGES TO PEACEBUILDING POST- SEPTEMBER 11TH

Recent peacebuilding efforts under UN auspices, such as those in Mozambique and East Timor, have been relatively successful, to the extent that 'the United Nations can justifiably claim that, if it is given support by the Security Council's member governments, it has the tools and the experience to take on other nation-building tasks in the future'.[33] Despite the relative success of such post-settlement peacebuilding initiatives, however, peacebuilding faces a new set of challenges, because of the effect of the events of 11 September 2001 in particular, for at least two reasons.

The first is the hostility to multilateralism generally, and the UN more particularly, on the part of the Bush administration, epitomised by Richard Perle's infamous farewell to the UN during the recent war against Iraq.[34] The second, related, reason is the revival of war as an instrument of foreign policy, undermining the commitment to 'international conflict management' as an alternative to the use of military force, again by the US administration (the Bush doctrine and 'pre-emptive strikes'). The events of 11 September 2001 provided the opportunity for these foreign policy doctrines to be implemented. Thus, the main challenge to peace-building as a form of 'conflict management' in the context of the current international situation is the resurrection of war as a deliberate instrument of foreign policy combined with the threat this poses to multilateralism, represented primarily by the UN.

The level of involvement of the international community in post-Taliban Afghanistan provides a stark contrast to the role of ONUMOZ and the UN in Mozambique, for example. In contrast to Mozambique (and East Timor), the UN has deliberately adopted a so-called 'light footprint' approach to Afghanistan, epitomised perhaps by the role of the

International Security Assistance Force (ISAF). ISAF, which is under NATO command but has a Security Council mandate, is restricted to protecting Kabul, leaving the warlords free to operate in the rest of the country, outside the control of the central, transitional government. Mahmood Monshipouri, for example, describes the government's 'limited control over large parts of the country, due to the abilities of regional warlords and armed factions', as 'alarming', from both a humanitarian and a peacebuilding perspective.[35]

According to Simon Chesterman, this contrast reflects the difference between peacebuilding, aimed at 'the basic peace and prosperity of the general population', and 'interventions ... justified in terms of narrow national interest'. 'This was reflected in the methods used by the United States to pursue its objectives in Afghanistan: by minimising the use of its own troops in favour of using Afghan proxies, more weapons were introduced into a country that was already heavily armed.'[36] At the very least, this does not fulfil peacebuilding's 'negative peace' requirements concerning the demobilisation of combatants and the decommissioning of weapons.

Similarly, the role of the UN in a post-Saddam Iraq remains in dispute, not least between the US and its ally Britain. The US wants to limit the UN to providing and distributing humanitarian assistance, while Britain has sought a stronger role for the UN in the post-Saddam governance of the country.[37] The August 2003 attack on the UN compound in Baghdad, which killed twenty-two people including the UN Secretary General's Special Representative Sergio Vieira de Mello, was a watershed event concerning the organisation's involvement in Iraq, and possibly its capacity to engage in large-scale reconstruction efforts in other post-conflict situations. The attack has been referred to as the UN's 'September 11th' because of its security implications for the organisation's operations worldwide. In this context, we must ask ourselves whether or not conflict prevention and peacebuilding can retain any relevance or promise as viable alternatives to war and armed conflict as apparently permanent features of international politics. Chesterman, for example, suggests that the two Iraq wars 'and the two Bush presidencies now provide bookends for the post-Cold War flirtation with a "new world order"',[38] in the form of a multilateral commitment to peacebuilding and international conflict management.

On the other hand, the difficulties experienced by the US and its allies in Iraq, and the disastrous impact of the invasion and occupation upon the civilian population, demonstrate the limits of armed intervention aimed at 'regime change' as a way of dealing with authoritarian governments responsible for widespread internal repression and human rights abuses.

These limits also apply to the 'war on terror' more generally, which appears increasingly to be an opportunity for the US to demonstrate its overwhelming military and political superiority rather than an effective way of dealing with the multiple threats to human security currently confronting us. There is perhaps a greater need now more than ever for multilateralism and international law (representing 'internationalism' and the institutional component of peacebuilding) and cosmopolitanism (as the expression of the values of human solidarity and the normative component of peacebuilding) as alternatives to the self-interested uni-lateralism of great power hegemony.

## V. PEACEBUILDING AS POLITICAL ENGINEERING

Some friendly critics of peacebuilding, such as Roland Paris, suggest that we need to 'challenge the conventional notion that peacebuilding is merely a technique for managing violence',[39] or a form of international conflict management. Thus, Paris argues that peacebuilding is a mechan-ism for transmitting Western values and institutions from the so-called developed world to so-called developing or emerging countries. In parti-cular, he writes that peacebuilding involves 'the globalisation of a particular model of domestic governance – liberal market democracy – from the core to the periphery of the international system'.[40]

One need only look at some of the characteristics of peacebuilding itemised in Table 10.1 to find support for this assertion. Also, Mozambique's success as an example of peacebuilding as effective 'international con-flict management' under UN auspices depends on processes of 'political engineering' initiated through a different set of multilateral institutions, that is, World Bank and IMF imposed structural adjustment programmes.[41]

Paris does acknowledge that in 'contrast to the old colonialism, peace-building missions have normally been deployed for limited periods, at the request of local parties, with the approval of international organisations, and with the goal of establishing conditions for war-shattered states to govern themselves'.[42] According to these criteria, peacebuilding con-trasts not merely with 'old colonialism', but also with current forms of imperial hegemony. We can ask, for example, how many of these criteria are currently being met in Iraq.

Nonetheless, he claims that peacebuilding missions, in addition to promoting Western norms and institutions, 'serve as vehicles for a parti-cular type of globalisation' of a specific model of the state, as a political unit with a centralised administration exercising exclusive authority over a bounded territory, 'or what is sometimes called the "Westphalian" state'.[43]

The form of globalisation associated with peacebuilding, then, includes not only the spread of liberal norms and institutions from the core of the international system to the periphery, but also the ongoing reproduction of the Westphalian state model.[44]

Thus, Ottaway and Lacina refer quite explicitly to UN peacebuilding missions as 'complex "nation building" (more accurately state reconstruction) tasks'.[45]

Attempts to establish such states may play an ambiguous role in the context of so-called 'new' or 'post-modern' wars, characterised as they are by disputes over state failure, state formation and state control, however. In other words, external efforts to establish a strong centralised state might exacerbate rather than alleviate or prevent social and political conflict in certain contexts. In such cases, it is the state itself that is in dispute, so that efforts to strengthen it merely augment a central feature of the armed conflict.

One can question the relevance of the Westphalian state to peacebuilding in Afghanistan, for instance, given that historically it has always had a weak central state but a strong society or social networks. Wimmer and Schetter, for example, claim 'for most Afghans the state represented an external entity, even a hostile one'. Effective state structures were restricted to a few urban centres, setting up an urban–rural divide that persisted into the twentieth century, during which these 'centres, especially Kabul, developed into oases of state rule'. This urban–rural, state–local division was an important feature of the civil war that began in the late 1970s.[46]

One consequence of this civil war, according to Wimmer and Schetter, is that even these 'embryonic state structures … collapsed at all levels', and it is in response to this chronic problem of state failure that they argue for state-building as a central component of reconstruction and peacebuilding in post-Taliban Afghanistan. In other words, in a situation characterised by warlordism, clientelism and the 'dissolution of territorial integrity', the appropriate response may be to focus on establishing a functioning state apparatus of some sort.[47] Thus, they suggest 'alongside the alleviation of immediate poverty, establishing institutions that are able to perform the basic functions of modern states should represent the main strategic goal of the reconstruction programme' in Afghanistan.[48]

To some extent, the difficulties associated with state-building reflect a tension between the two components of peacebuilding identified in *An Agenda for Peace*: post-settlement reconstruction (or positive peace) and violence prevention (or negative peace). State- or institution-building is an important element of post-settlement reconstruction, while conflict resolution capacities in the broadest sense are important for sustaining the cessation of armed conflict and maintaining the process of 'Clausewitz in reverse'. In other words, in some contexts activities aimed at achieving positive peace, such as state- or nation-building, may undermine the conditions required for achieving negative peace, through entrenching existing political divisions and disputes and pre-empting or preventing processes of dialogue, mediation, negotiation, and so on.

A premature emphasis on the formal aspects of state-building in the form of multiparty elections and power-sharing arrangements, for example, may threaten or pre-empt efforts aimed at developing indigenous capacities or approaches to ending armed conflict. Paris claims, for instance, that in Rwanda 'plans for political liberalization and democratic elections … contributed to the collapse of a fragile peace', culminating ultimately in the genocide of 1994.[49] He argues, more generally, that international efforts to insert a particular model of the state and society, liberal market democracy, into war-affected countries 'gave rise to unanticipated and destabilizing side effects in several of the states that hosted peacebuilding missions'.[50]

Thus, the danger associated with a narrow interpretation of state-building, from a peacebuilding perspective, is not only that it can represent an undue imposition of Western values and institutions, but also that it can aggravate rather than ameliorate existing social and political tensions. From a peacebuilding perspective, political institutions are required that can manage the process of 'Clausewitz in reverse', whether or not these conform to Western ideals or the Westphalian model of the state. The process of state-building must be understood in this broad sense, rather than as some Western import, if it is to contribute positively to post-war peacebuilding.

The underlying point is that peacebuilding must be seen as more than a technical exercise in international conflict management, which can be implemented with predictable success so long as sufficient resources and expertise are provided. Many of the values and norms implicit in peace-building as a multilateral enterprise are reflected in its focus on liberal market democracy as the model of state and society that provides the key to peace for war-torn countries, both domestically and internationally. A central objective of establishing political institutions as a component of peacebuilding, however, must be to support peaceful methods of dealing with social and political conflict based on indigenous capacities for conflict resolution, which may or may not conform to Western ideals or interests. This caveat concerning the translation of shared norms or values into particular political and economic institutions or structures must also be applied to the cosmopolitan component or impetus behind peace-building as a multilateral activity.

Peacebuilding is a multidimensional activity involving a combination of post-settlement reconstruction and violence prevention. As such, a comprehensive approach to peacebuilding will include a concern with positive peace, or distributive and procedural justice, and negative peace, or the cessation of armed threats to a population's wellbeing and survival, achieved by nonviolent methods such as processes of conflict resolution, mediation, negotiation, and so on.

In the post-Cold War era, the UN has played a leading role in some relatively successful instances of peacebuilding, in Mozambique and East Timor for example, indicating the viability of such initiatives as a form of international assistance to countries emerging out of armed conflict. Recent changes in US foreign policy, however, in the wake of the events of 11 September 2001 provide a serious challenge to peacebuilding as an effective multilateral instrument. At a more profound level, peace-building may be a vehicle for the globalisation of certain values and institutions, especially those associated with the liberal market state. This emphasis on state-building must not be allowed to undermine other crucial aspects of peacebuilding, converting it into a process of externally-imposed political engineering masquerading as a technical exercise in international conflict management.

This discussion of peacebuilding has touched on two themes that have recurred throughout this book. The first concerns the ambivalent contri-bution of the state towards the peaceful resolution of armed conflict, because the state itself can be a focus of and a mechanism for political violence. The second concerns the importance of cosmopolitan values, epitomised by the normative component of peacebuilding (cf. Table 10.1) and its commitment to nonviolent processes of social and political change, in providing the moral impetus for finding alternatives to war and armed conflict as ways of dealing with social and political conflict. We must ensure, however, that these cosmopolitan values, like peacebuilding itself, are not just a vehicle for the imposition of Western norms and institutions on vulnerable societies in other parts of the world. Thus, peacebuilding as an alternative to war and political violence reveals that genuine cosmopolitanism involves equal respect for all human beings whatever their particular social and political context.

## NOTES

1. Ottaway and Lacina, 'International Interventions and Imperialism', p. 77.
2. See Galtung, 'Three Approaches to Peace', pp. 282–304.
3. Boutros-Ghali, *An Agenda for Peace*, p. 11.
4. Ottaway and Lacina, 'International Interventions and Imperialism', p. 76.
5. Boutros-Ghali, *An Agenda for Peace*, p. 11.

6. Ottaway and Lacina, 'International Interventions and Imperialism', p. 82.
7. See Kaldor, *New and Old Wars*, for example.
8. Annan, 'Executive Summary', p. 3.
9. Kaldor, *New and Old Wars*, p. 123.
10. Galtung, 'Violence, Peace and Peace Research', pp. 616–28.
11. As cited in Peu, 'The UN, Peacekeeping and Collective Human Security', p. 53.
12. Ramsbotham, 'Reflections on UN Post-Settlement Peacebuilding', p. 172.
13. Lerche, 'Peace Building through Reconciliation', p. 66.
14. Ibid. p. 74.
15. Small, 'Peacebuilding in Postconflict Societies', p. 78.
16. See ibid. pp. 78–80.
17. Catholic Relief Services, 'Sixteen Categories of Peacebuilding Activities', pp. 183–7.
18. Ramsbotham, 'Reflections on UN Post-Settlement Peacebuilding', p. 182. Last, 'Organizing for Effective Peacebuilding', p. 86.
19. International Conference Towards Better Peace Building Practice, 'Annex 3: Gender and Peacebuilding', p. 220.
20. Lerche, 'Peace Building through Reconciliation', p. 71.
21. International Conference Towards Better Peace Building Practice, 'Annex 3: Gender and Peacebuilding', p. 221.
22. Porter, 'Women, Political Decision-Making, and Peace-Building', p. 246.
23. Ibid. p. 249.
24. International Conference Towards Better Peace Building Practice, 'Annex 3: Gender and Peacebuilding', p. 223. See also Porter, 'Women, Political Decision-Making, and Peace-Building'.
25. Ajello, 'Mozambique: Implementation of the 1992 Peace Agreement', p. 615.
26. Instituto del Tercer Mundo, 'Mozambique', p. 408.
27. Ajello, 'Mozambique: Implementation of the 1992 Peace Agreement', p. 621.
28. Ibid. p. 622.
29. Ibid. p. 622.
30. Ibid. p. 631.
31. See Federici, 'War, Globalization, and Reproduction', p. 158ff.
32. Paris, 'International peacebuilding', p. 649.
33. Steele, 'Nation Building in East Timor', p. 86.
34. Perle, 'It's over for the UN and good riddance', p. 12.
35. Monshipouri, 'NGOs and Peacebuilding in Afghanistan', pp. 142–3.
36. Chesterman, 'Bush, the United Nations and Nation-building', p. 104.
37. See ibid. p. 105.
38. Ibid. p. 110.
39. Paris, 'International peacebuilding', p. 655.
40. Ibid. p. 638.
41. Cf. ibid. pp. 648–9.
42. Ibid. p. 652.
43. Ibid. p. 654.
44. Ibid. p. 655.
45. Ottaway and Lacina, 'International Interventions and Imperialism', pp. 79–80.
46. Wimmer and Schetter, 'Putting State-Formation First', p. 528.
47. Ibid. p. 528ff.
48. Ibid. p. 534.
49. Paris, 'Wilson's Ghost', p. 768.
50. Ibid. p. 766.

# CHAPTER 11

# CONCLUSION

The purpose of this book has been three-fold. Firstly, it has compared the implications of three theories of the role of ethics in international politics (political realism, internationalism and cosmopolitanism) for the moral problems associated with war and the use of armed force. Secondly, it has connected these three theories to two specific positions on the morality of armed force: just war theory and pacifism. And thirdly, it has applied this largely ethical and theoretical discussion to some contemporary problems of armed conflict, in the form of new or post-modern wars. In particular, it has tried to assess specific strategies for dealing with contemporary armed conflict, such as human security, humanitarian intervention and peacebuilding, from a cosmopolitan perspective.

One of the patterns revealed by these different levels of discussion has been the complexity of the relationships between more general theories concerning the role of ethics in international politics, and specific moral positions concerning the use of armed force. At first glance, for example, there appears to be a superficial connection between internationalism and just war theory, and between cosmopolitanism and pacifism. It has been said, for example, that international law had its origins in attempts to translate just war criteria into specific, judicable principles of jurisprudence. Also, much of the modern just war discourse is quite state-centred, in accordance with internationalism's commitment to the principle of state sovereignty as a central feature of international order. Similarly, cosmopolitanism and pacifism seem to share a fundamental commitment to the equal value of every human life.

On the other hand, just war theory has its cosmopolitan element in the form of the *jus in bello* principle of noncombatant immunity, for example, which makes no distinction between 'enemy' and 'allied' civilians. This cosmopolitan just war principle, furthermore, has been embodied in international humanitarian law through state-signed treaties and conventions. It seems, then, that cosmopolitanism and internationalism can be complementary, rather than contradictory, positions when it comes to the ethics of peace and war.

157

Thus the attitude of cosmopolitanism towards both internationalism and just war theory seems to be determined by additional or deeper debates at the level of both political theory (concerning the nature of the state) and normative ethics (concerning the pacifist prohibition against killing in particular). Kantian cosmopolitanism, for example, sees its commitment to a universal moral community as complementary to and perhaps reinforced by the rule of law both domestically and internationally via liberal democratic governments. More radical or revolutionary versions of cosmopolitanism (such as Tolstoyan pacifism), on the other hand, oppose the state precisely because it embodies the institutionalisation and legitimisation of political violence against human beings.

Thus, a key theme of the book is the ambivalence of cosmopolitanism to the state and to the use of armed force. These issues are linked because of the state's role in legitimising the use of violence.

From a Kantian cosmopolitan perspective, perhaps the best contribution cosmopolitanism can make is at the levels of norms and values, in the form of the human security paradigm perhaps. Choices about the best political strategy for implementing and institutionalising these values, on the other hand, must be context-specific. In the case of 'state failure' conflicts, for example, state-building may play a crucial role in achieving peace, stability and human security. In other contexts, however, such as 'state control' conflicts, multilateral institutions and civil society organisations may play a much stronger role in reining in authoritarian state practices. The important point is that these political strategies acquire credibility and legitimacy because of their connection with cosmopolitan norms and values such as human rights, human development and human security.

The issue of humanitarian intervention reveals the tension between pacifist prohibitions against the taking of human life and our cosmopolitan responsibility to protect it. This tension could be called 'the pacifist dilemma'. The cosmopolitan responsibility to protect human life raises two further questions, however. We must clarify the extent to which, firstly, it permits us to kill combatants, and secondly, to place noncombatant lives at risk in the context of the use of armed force. It would seem that the just war theory provides answers to these questions in a way that pacifism does not, in the form of its two *jus in bello* criteria, proportionality and discrimination, in particular. Just war theory, in other words, provides criteria for balancing our sometimes competing obligations not to take human life while at the same time doing our utmost to protect it, through defining moral limits to the use of armed force.

The only counterargument of the revolutionary pacifist would seem to be to query the advantages of the militarised state as a way of dealing with the problems of political and social conflict, including aggressive threats to human life. In other words, if the debate occurs solely at the level of ethics, the pacifist is left with a dilemma, or two competing sets of moral obligations, that may be more easily resolved by just war theory. Pacifism, which at the outset seemed to be primarily a moral position concerning the taking of human life, may be at it strongest and most distinctive when it queries the role and impact of the state from within political theory.

In summary then, there are two essential challenges confronting cosmopolitanism when it is applied to the ethics of peace and war. At the level of normative ethics, cosmopolitanism must address the pacifist dilemma generated by our competing obligations not to take human life while at the same time doing our utmost to protect it. At the level of political theory, it must deal with the state as either the enemy or an instrument of cosmopolitan norms and values.

Thus, at the end of this discussion we must be aware of two things. We must accept the complexity of the relationships between theories about the role of ethics in international relations more generally and just war theory and pacifism as rival moral positions concerning the use of armed force. We must also acknowledge the inadequacy of cosmopolitanism on its own to provide a clear and unambiguous response to the moral and political problems associated with war and armed conflict, without further exploring issues in both normative ethics and political theory.

# BIBLIOGRAPHY

Adebajo, A. and Sriram, C. L. (eds) (2001), *Managing Armed Conflicts*, London: Frank Cass.

Ajello, A. (1999), 'Mozambique: Implementation of the 1992 Peace Agreement', in Crocker, Hampson and Aall, *Herding Cats: Multiparty Mediation in a Complex World*.

Almond, B. and Hill, D. (eds) (1991), *Applied Philosophy: Morals and Metaphysics in Contemporary Debate*, London: Routledge.

Annan, K. (2001), 'Executive Summary', *Report of the Secretary-General: Prevention of armed conflict*, UN (A/55/985–S/2002/574).

Archibugi, D. (1998), 'Principles of Cosmopolitan Democracy', in Archibugi, Held and Köhler, *Re-imagining Political Community: Studies in Cosmopolitan Democracy*.

Archibugi, D., Held, D. and Köhler, M. (eds) (1998), *Re-imagining Political Community: Studies in Cosmopolitan Democracy*, Cambridge: Polity Press.

Archibugi, D. (2004), 'Cosmopolitan Democracy', *The CSD Bulletin*, Vol. 11, No. 1.

Armon, J. and Philipson, L. (eds) (1998), *Accord: Demanding Sacrifice – War and Negotiation in Sri Lanka*, London: Conciliation Resources.

Auvinen, J. and Kivimäki, T. (2000), 'Somalia: The Struggle for Resources', in Nafziger, Stewart and Väyrynen, *War, Hunger, and Displacement: The Origins of Humanitarian Emergencies, Volume 2: Case Studies*.

Axworthy, L. (2001), 'Introduction', in McRae and Hubert, *Human Security and the New Diplomacy: Protecting People, Promoting Peace*.

Bajpai, K. (2000), 'The Idea of a Human Security Audit', *The Joan B. Kroc Institute for International Peace Studies Report*, No. 19.

Barry, B. (1998), 'International Society from a Cosmopolitan Perspective', in Mapel and Nardin, *International Society: Diverse Ethical Perspectives*.

Baylis, J. (1997), 'International Security in the Post-Cold War Era', in Smith and Baylis, *The Globalization of World Politics: An Introduction to International Relations*.

Beetham, D. (1998), 'Human Rights as a Model for Cosmopolitan Democracy', in Archibugi, Held and Köhler, *Re-imagining Political Community: Studies in Cosmopolitan Democracy*.

Beitz, C. R. (1999), 'Social and Cosmopolitan Liberalism', *International Affairs*, Vol. 75, No. 3.

Bellamy, A. J. (2003), 'Humanitarian Intervention and the Three Traditions', *Global Society*, Vol. 17, No. 1.

Bellamy, A. J. (2004), 'Ethics and Intervention: The "Humanitarian Exception" and the Problem of Abuse in the Case of Iraq', *Journal of Peace Research*, Vol. 41, No. 2.

Bennett, S. (2000), 'Socialist Pacifism and Nonviolent Social Revolution: The War

Resisters League and The Spanish Civil War, 1936–1939', *Peace & Change*, Vol. 25, No. 1.

Bohman, J. and Lutz-Bachman, M. (1997) 'Introduction', in Bohman and Lutz-Bachman, *Perpetual Peace: Essays on Kant's Cosmopolitan Ideal*.

Bohman, J. and Lutz-Bachman, M. (eds) (1997), *Perpetual Peace: Essays on Kant's Cosmopolitan Ideal*, Cambridge, MA: The MIT Press.

Boutros-Ghali, B. (1992), *An Agenda for Peace*, New York: United Nations.

Brock, P., *Varieties of Pacifism: A Survey from Antiquity to the Outset of the Twentieth Century*, Syracuse, NY: Syracuse University Press.

Brock, P. and Young, N. (1999), *Pacifism in the Twentieth Century*, Syracuse, NY: Syracuse University Press.

Brown, C. (1992), *International Relations Theory: New Normative Approaches*, London: Harvester Wheatsheaf.

Brown, G. D. (2003), 'Proportionality and Just War', *Journal of Military Ethics*, Vol. 2, No. 3.

Buchanan, A. and Keohane, R. O. (2004), 'The Preventive Use of Force: A Cosmopolitan Institutional Proposal', *Ethics & International Affairs*, Vol. 18, No. 1.

Bull, H. (1992), *The Anarchical Society: A Study of Order in World Politics*, London: Macmillan.

Bull, H. (1994) 'Martin Wight and the theory of international relations', in Wight, *International Theory: The Three Traditions*.

Bullion, A. (2002), 'Dreaming of a War-Free Future', *The World Today*, Vol. 58, No. 12.

Cady, D. L. (1989), *From Warism to Pacifism: A Moral Continuum*, Philadelphia: Temple University Press.

Calhoun, L. (2002), 'How Violence Breeds Violence: Some Utilitarian Considerations', *Politics*, Vol. 22, No. 2.

Carr, E. H. (1946), *The Twenty Years' Crisis 1919–1939: An Introduction to the Study of International Relations*, 2nd edn, New York: Harper & Row.

Catholic Relief Services (2002), 'Sixteen Categories of Peacebuilding Activities', in Galama and van Tongeren, *Towards Better Peacebuilding Practice: On Lessons Learned, Evaluation Practices and Aid and Conflict*.

Ceadel, M. (1989), *Thinking about Peace and War*, Oxford and New York: Oxford University Press.

Charvet, J. (1998), 'The Possibility of a Cosmopolitan Ethical Order Based on the Idea of Universal Human Rights', *Millennium: Journal of International Studies*, Vol. 27, No. 3.

Chesterman, S. (2001), *Just War or Just Peace? Humanitarian intervention and international law*, Oxford: Oxford University Press.

Chesterman, S. (2004), 'Bush, the United Nations and Nation-building', *Survival*, Vol. 46, No. 1.

Chomsky, N. (1999), *The New Military Humanism: Lessons from Kosovo*, London: Pluto Press.

Coates, A. J. (1997), *The Ethics of War*, Manchester: Manchester University Press.

Cochran, M. (1999), *Normative Theory in International Relations: A Pragmatic Approach*, Cambridge: Cambridge University Press.

Commission on Human Security (2001a), 'Plan for Establishment of the Commission on Human Security', 24 January 2001, www.humansecurity-chs.org/about/pressrelease. html

Commission on Human Security (2001b), 'Establishment of the Commission', www.humansecurity-chs.org/about/Establishment. html

Commission on Human Security (2003a), 'Outline of the Report of the Commission on Human Security', www.humansecurity-chs.org/ finalreport/outline.html

Commission on Human Security (2003b), 'Press Release', www. humansecurity-chs.org/ finalreport/pressrelease.html

Cook, R. (2000), 'Guiding Humanitarian Intervention', www.fco.gov.uk/ news/speechtext.

Crocker, C. A., Hampson, F. O. and Aall, P. (eds) (1999), *Herding Cats: Multiparty Mediation in a Complex World*, Washington, DC: United States Institute of Peace Press.

Crocker, C. A., Hampson, F. O. and Aall, P. (eds) (2001), *Turbulent Peace: The Challenges of Managing International Conflict*, Washington, DC: United States Institute of Peace Press.

de Jonge Oudraat, C. (2000) 'Humanitarian Intervention: The Lessons Learned', *Current History*.

Dower, N. (1998), *World Ethics: The New Agenda*, Edinburgh: Edinburgh University Press.

Dower, N. (2002), 'Global Citizenship and Peace', in Dower and Williams, *Global Citizenship: A Critical Introduction*.

Dower, N. and Williams, J. (eds) (2002), *Global Citizenship: A Critical Introduction*, New York: Routledge.

Dunne, T. (1997), 'Liberalism', in Smith and Baylis, *The Globalization of World Politics: An Introduction to International Relations*.

Dunne, T. (1997), 'Realism', in Smith and Baylis, *The Globalization of World Politics: An Introduction to International Relations*.

Dunne, T. and Wheeler, N. J. (2004), '"We the Peoples": Contending Discourses of Security in Human Rights Theory and Practice', *International Relations*, Vol. 18, No. 1.

Erasmus, D. [1513] (1966), 'Letter to Anthony a Bergis', in Mayer, *The Pacifist Conscience*.

Erskine, T. (2000), 'Embedded Cosmopolitanism and the Case of War: Restraint, Discrimination and Overlapping Communities', *Global Society*, Vol. 14, No. 4.

Erskine, T. (2002), '"Citizen of nowhere" or "the point where circles intersect"? Impartialist and embedded cosmopolitanisms', *Review of International Studies*, Vol. 28, No. 3.

Falk, R. (2004), 'A New Gandhian Moment?', *Resurgence*, No. 222.

Federici, S. (2000), 'War, Globalization, and Reproduction', *Peace & Change*, Vol. 25, No. 2.

Fernando, M. (2002), 'Root Causes of Ethnic Conflict and Attempted Peace Initiatives in Sri Lanka', *SangSaeng*, Vol. 3.

Fixdal, M. and Smith, D. (1998), 'Humanitarian Intervention and Just War', *Mershon International Studies Review*, Vol. 42, No. 2.

Franke, M. F. N. (1995), 'Immanuel Kant and the (Im)Possibility of International Relations Theory', *Alternatives*, Vol. 20, No. 3.

Frost, M. (1996), *Ethics in International Relations: A Constitutive Theory*, Cambridge: Cambridge University Press.

Galama, A. and van Tongeren, P. (eds) (2002), *Towards Better Peacebuilding Practice: On Lessons Learned, Evaluation Practices and Aid and Conflict*, Utrecht: European Centre for Conflict Prevention.

Galtung, J. (1969), 'Violence, Peace and Peace Research', *Journal of Peace Research*, Vol. 6, No. 3.

Galtung, J. (1975), 'Three Approaches to Peace: Peacekeeping, Peacemaking and Peace-building', in Galtung, *Peace, War and Defence – Essays in Peace Research Vol. 2*.

Galtung, J. (1975), *Peace, War and Defence – Essays in Peace Research Vol. 2*, Copenhagen: Christian Ejlers.

Golberg, E. and Hubert, D. (2001), 'Case Study: The Security Council and the Protection of Civilians', in McRae and Hubert, *Human Security and the New Diplomacy: Protecting People, Promoting Peace.*

Goodhand, J. and Hulme, D. (1999), 'From wars to complex political emergencies: understanding conflict and peace-building in the new world disorder', *Third World Quarterly*, Vol. 20, No. 1.

Habermas, J. (1997), 'Kant's Idea of Perpetual Peace, with the Benefit of Two Hundred Years' Hindsight', in Bohman and Lutz-Bachman, *Perpetual Peace: Essays on Kant's Cosmopolitan Ideal.*

Hampson, F. O. (2002), *Madness in the Multitude: Human Security and World Disorder*, Don Mills, Ontario: Oxford University Press.

Harris, G. and Lewis, N. (1999), 'Armed Conflict in Developing Countries: Extent, nature and causes', in Harris (ed.), *Recovery from Armed Conflict in Developing Countries.*

Harris, G. (ed.) (1999), *Recovery from Armed Conflict in Developing Countries*, London and New York: Routledge.

Hataley, T. S. and Nossal, K. R. (2004), 'The Limits of the Human Security Agenda: The Case of Canada's Response to the Timor Crisis', *Global Change, Peace & Security*, Vol. 16, No. 1.

Held, D. (1997), 'Cosmopolitan Democracy and the Global Order: A New Agenda', in Bohman and Lutz-Bachman, *Perpetual Peace: Essays on Kant's Cosmopolitan Ideal.*

Held, D. (2003), 'Cosmopolitanism: globalisation tamed?', *Review of International Studies*, Vol. 29, No. 4.

Hoffman, S. (2001), 'The Debate about Intervention', in Crocker, Hampson and Aall, *Turbulent Peace: The Challenges of Managing International Conflict.*

Holliday, I. (2002), 'When is a cause just?', *Review of International Studies*, Vol. 28, No. 3.

Holliday, I. (2003), 'Ethics of Intervention: Just War theory and the Challenge of the 21st Century', *International Relations*, Vol. 17, No. 2.

Holmes, R. L. (1989), *On War and Morality*, Princeton: Princeton University Press.

Honneth, A. (1997), 'Is Universalism a Moral Trap? The Presuppositions and Limits of a Politics of Human Rights', in Bohman and Lutz-Bachman, *Perpetual Peace: Essays on Kant's Cosmopolitan Ideal.*

Howard, M. (1999), 'When Are Wars Decisive?', *Survival*, Vol. 41, No. 1.

Hubert, D. and Bonser, M. (2001), 'Humanitarian Military Intervention', in McRae and Hubert, *Human Security and the New Diplomacy: Protecting People, Promoting Peace.*

Instituto del Tercer Mundo (1999), 'Mozambique', *The World Guide 1999/2000: A View from the South*, Oxford: New Internationalist Publications.

International Commission on Intervention and State Sovereignty (2001), *The Responsibility to Protect*, Ottawa: International Development Research Centre.

International Conference Towards Better Peace Building Practice (2002), 'Annex 3: Gender and Peacebuilding', in Galama and van Tongeren, *Towards Better Peacebuilding Practice: On Lessons Learned, Evaluation Practices and Aid and Conflict.*

Kaldor, M. (1996), 'A Cosmopolitan Response to New Wars', *Peace Review*, Vol. 8, No. 4.

Kaldor, M. (1997), 'Introduction' to Kaldor and Vashee, *Restructuring the Global Military Sector, Volume 1: New Wars.*

Kaldor, M. and Vashee, B. (eds) (1997), *Restructuring the Global Military Sector, Volume 1: New Wars*, London and Washington: Pinter.

Kaldor, M. (1999), *New and Old Wars: Organized Violence in a Global Era*, Cambridge: Polity Press.

Kant, I. [1795] (1992), 'To Perpetual Peace: A Philosophical Sketch', in *Perpetual Peace and other essays on politics, history, and morals*, Indianapolis: Hackett Publishing Company.

Kaufman, W. (2003), 'What is the Scope of Civilian Immunity in Wartime?', *Journal of Military Ethics*, Vol. 2, No. 3.

Keen, D. (2001), 'Sudan: Conflict and Rationality', in Stewart and Valpy Fitzgerald and Associates (eds), *War and Underdevelopment, Volume II: Country Experiences*.

King, G. and Murray, C. J. L. (2001–2), 'Rethinking Human Security', *Political Science Quarterly*, Vol. 116, No. 4.

Kloos, P. (2002), 'A turning point? From civil struggle to civil war in Sri Lanka', in Schmidt and Schröder, *Anthropology of Violence and Conflict*.

Knudsen, T. B. (1997), 'Humanitarian Intervention Revisited: Post-Cold War Responses to Classical Problems', in Pugh, *The UN, Peace and Force*.

Krippendorff, E. (2002), 'The state and militarism after 11 September', *Peace News*, No. 2447.

Küng, H. (2002), 'A Global Ethic for a New Global Order', in Dower and Williams, *Global Citizenship: A Critical Introduction*.

Last, D. (2000), 'Organizing for Effective Peacebuilding', in Woodhouse and Ramsbotham, *Peacekeeping and Conflict Resolution*.

Latham, A. (2002), 'Warfare Transformed: A Braudelian Perspective on the "Revolution in Military Affairs"', *European Journal of International Relations*, Vol. 8, No. 2.

Lerche, C. (2000), 'Peace Building through Reconciliation', *International Journal of Peace Studies*, Vol. 5, No. 2.

Linklater, A. (2002), 'The problem of harm in world politics: implications for the sociology of states-systems', *International Affairs*, Vol. 78, No. 2.

Macgregor, G. H. C. (2000), 'The relevance of an impossible ideal', in Wink, *Peace is the Way: Writings on Nonviolence from the Fellowship of Reconciliation*.

Mapel, D. R. and Nardin, T. (eds) (1998), *International Society: Diverse Ethical Perspectives*, Princeton: Princeton University Press.

Mayer, P. (1966), 'Introduction' to Mayer, *The Pacifist Conscience*.

Mayer, P. (ed.) (1966), *The Pacifist Conscience*, Harmondsworth: Penguin Books.

McRae, R. (2001a), 'Conclusion: International Relations and the New Diplomacy', in McRae and Hubert, *Human Security and the New Diplomacy: Protecting People, Promoting Peace*.

McRae, R. (2001b), 'Human Security in a Globalized World', in McRae and Hubert, *Human Security and the New Diplomacy: Protecting People, Promoting Peace*.

McRae, R. and Hubert, D. (eds) (2001), *Human Security and the New Diplomcay: Protecting People, Promoting Peace*, Montreal and Kingston: McGill-Queen's University Press.

McSweeney, B. (1999), *Security, Identity and Interests: A Sociology of International Relations*, Cambridge: Cambridge University Press.

Monshipouri, M. (2003), 'NGOs and Peacebuilding in Afghanistan', *International Peacekeeping*, Vol. 10, No. 1.

Morgenthau, H. (1978), *Politics Among Nations: The Struggle for Power and Peace*, 5th edn, New York: Alfred A. Knopf.

Mueller, J. (2000), 'The Banality of "Ethnic War"', *International Security*, Vol. 25, No. 1.

Mueller, J. (2003), 'Policing the Remnants of War', *Journal of Peace Research*, Vol. 40, No. 5.

Müllerson, R. (2002), '*Jus Ad Bellum*: Plus Ça Change (Le Monde) Plus C'est La Même Chose (Le Droit)?', *Journal of Conflict and Security Law*, Vol. 7, No. 2.

Nafziger, E. W., Stewart, F. and Väyrynen, R. (eds) (2000), *War, Hunger, and Displacement: The Origins of Humanitarian Emergencies, Volume 2: Case Studies*, Oxford: Oxford University Press.

Nardin, T. (2002), 'The Moral Basis of Humanitarian Intervention', *Ethics & International Affairs*, Vol. 16, No. 1.

Newman, E. and Schnabel A. (eds) (2002), *Recovering from Civil Conflict: Reconciliation, Peace and Development*, London: Frank Cass.

Niebuhr, R. (1960), *Moral Man and Immoral Society: A Study in Ethics and Politics*, New York: Charles Scribner's Sons.

Nissan, E. (1998), 'Historical Context', in Armon and Philipson (eds), *Accord: Demanding Sacrifice – War and Negotiation in Sri Lanka*.

Norman, R. (1991) 'The Case for Pacifism', in Almond and Hill, *Applied Philosophy: Morals and Metaphysics in Contemporary Debate*.

Norman, R. (1995), *Ethics, Killing and War*, Cambridge: Cambridge University Press.

Nussbaum, M. C. (1997), 'Kant and Cosmopolitanism', in Bohman and Lutz-Bachman, *Perpetual Peace: Essays on Kant's Cosmopolitan Ideal*.

Ottaway, M. and Lacina, B. (2003), 'International Interventions and Imperialism: Lessons from the 1990s', *SAIS Review*, Vol. 13, No. 2.

Paris, R. (2001), 'Wilson's Ghost: The Faulty Assumptions of Postconflict Peacebuilding', in Crocker, Hampson and Aall, *Turbulent Peace: The Challenges of Managing International Conflict*.

Paris, R. (2002), 'International peacebuilding and the "mission civilisatrice"', *Review of International Studies*, Vol. 28, No. 4.

Perle, R. (2003), 'It's over for the UN and good riddance', *The Irish Times*, 22 March.

Peu, S. (2002), 'The UN, Peacekeeping and Collective Human Security: From *An Agenda for Peace* to the Brahimi Report', in Newman and Schnabel, *Recovering from Civil Conflict: Reconciliation, Peace and Development*.

PoKempner, D. (2003), 'Bending the Rules', *The World Today*, Vol. 59, No. 5.

Porter, E. (2003), 'Women, Political Decision-Making, and Peace-Building', *Global Change, Peace & Security*, Vol. 15, No. 3.

Project Ploughshares (1997), *Armed Conflicts Report 1997*, Waterloo, Ontario: Project Ploughshares.

Pugh, M. (ed.) (1997), *The UN, Peace and Force*, London: Frank Cass.

Ramcharan, B. (2004), 'Human rights and human security', *Disarmament Forum*, No. 1.

Ramsbotham, O. (2000), 'Reflections on UN Post-Settlement Peacebuilding', in Woodhouse and Ramsbotham, *Peacekeeping and Conflict Resolution*.

Rawls, J. (1973), *A Theory of Justice*, Oxford: Oxford University Press.

Robinson, M. (2000), 'Development and rights: the undeniable nexus', United Nations Office of the High Commissioner for Human Rights.

Rodin, D. (2002), *War and Self-Defense*, Oxford: Oxford University Press.

Rogers, P. (2002), *Losing Control: Global Security in the Twenty-first Century*, 2nd edn, London: Pluto Press.

Rupesinghe, K. and Mumtaz, K. (eds) (1996), *Internal Conflicts in South Asia*, London: Sage.

Russell, B. (1915), 'The Ethics of War', *The International Journal of Ethics*, Vol. 15, No. 2.

Russell, B. (1917), 'War and Non-Resistance', in *Justice in War-Time*, Nottingham: Spokesman Books.

Russell, B. [1959] (1966) 'Inconsistency?', in Mayer, *The Pacifist Conscience.*

Russell, B. [1951] (1966), 'Man's Peril', in Mayer, *The Pacifist Conscience.*

Saravanamuttu, P. (2003), 'Sri Lanka: the best and last chance for peace?', *Conflict, Security & Development*, Vol. 3, No. 1.

Schmidt, B. E. and Schröder, I. W. (eds) (2001), *Anthropology of Violence and Conflict*, London and New York: Routledge.

Scott, S. V. (2004), *International Law in World Politics: An Introduction*, Boulder, CO and London: Lynne Rienner Publishers.

Shapcott, R. (2002), 'Cosmopolitan Conversations: Justice Dialogue and the Cosmo-politan Project', *Global Society*, Vol. 16, No. 3.

Small, M. (2001), 'Peacebuilding in Postconflict Societies', in McRae and Hubert, *Human Security and the New Diplomacy: Protecting People, Promoting Peace.*

Smith, M. L. R. (2003), 'Guerillas in the mist: reassessing strategy and low intensity warfare', *Review of International Studies*, Vol. 29, No. 1.

Smith, S. (1997), 'New Approaches to International Theory', in Smith and Baylis, *The Globalization of World Politics: An Introduction to International Relations.*

Smith, S. and Baylis, J. (eds) (1997), *The Globalization of World Politics: An Introduction to International Relations*, Oxford: Oxford University Press.

Spini, D. (2002), 'Reflections on Death, Fear and Security', *Security Dialogue*, Vol. 33, No. 4.

Steele, J. (2002), 'Nation Building in East Timor', *World Policy Journal*, Vol. 19, No. 2.

Stevenson, N. (2002), 'Cosmopolitanism and the Future of Democracy: Politics, Culture and the Self', *New Political Economy*, Vol. 7, No. 2.

Stewart, F. and Valpy Fitzgerald and Associates (eds) (2001), *War and Under-development, Volume II: Country Experiences*, Oxford: Oxford University Press.

Tolstoy, L. [1902] (1966), 'Letter to a Non-commissioned Officer', in Mayer, *The Pacifist Conscience.*

United Nations Development Programme (1994), *Human Development Report 1994*, New York: Oxford University Press.

Uyangoda, J. (1996), 'Militarization, Violent State, Violent Society: Sri Lanka', in Rupesinghe and Mumtaz, *Internal Conflicts in South Asia.*

Walzer, M. (1992), *Just and Unjust Wars: A Moral Argument with Historical Illustrations*, 2nd edn, New York: HarperCollins.

Wendt, A. (1992), 'Anarchy is what states make of it: the social construction of power politics', *International Organisation*, Vol. 46, No. 2.

Wheeler, N. J. (2000), *Saving Strangers: Humanitarian Intervention in International Society*, Oxford: Oxford University Press.

Wheeler, N. J. (2001), 'Review Article – Humanitarian Intervention after Kosovo: Emergent Norm, Moral Duty or the Coming Anarchy?', *International Affairs*, Vol. 17, No. 1.

Wheeler, N. J. (2002), 'Dying for "Enduring Freedom": Accepting Responsibility for Civilian Casualties in the War against Terrorism', *International Relations*, Vol. 16, No. 2.

Wight, M. (1994), *International Theory: The Three Traditions*, London: Leicester University Press.

Wimmer, A. and Schetter, C. (2003), 'Putting State-Formation First: Some Recommendations for Reconstruction and Peace-Making in Afghanistan', *Journal of International Development*, Vol. 15, No. 5.

Wink, W. (ed.) (2000), *Peace is the Way: Writings on Nonviolence from the Fellowship of Reconciliation*, Maryknoll, NY: Orbis Books.

Woodhouse, T. and Ramsbotham, O. (eds) (2000), *Peacekeeping and Conflict Resolution*, London: Frank Cass.

Young, N. (1999), 'Preface', in Brock and Young, *Pacifism in the Twentieth Century*.

Zack-Williams, T. (2000), 'The Forgotten Realities of Contemporary Africa', *New Political Economy*, Vol. 5, No. 1.

Zahar, M.-J. (2001), 'Protégés, Clients, Cannon Fodder: Civilians in the Calculus of Militias', in Adebajo and Sriram, *Managing Armed Conflicts*.

# INDEX

Afghanistan, 27–8, 37, 106, 107, 118,
    150–1, 153
Africa *see* Mozambique; Rwanda;
    Somalia; Sudan
African Peace Facility, 118
*Agenda for Peace, An* (United Nations),
    142, 144, 145, 153
aggression, 63, 65
Al Qaeda, 37, 67, 105
anarchy: and sovereign states, 21
Annan, Kofi, 113, 143
antimilitarism *see* pacifism; socialist
    antimilitarism
Archibugi, Daniele, 47, 50–1, 127
armed conflicts, 5, 37, 52, 93–7; *see also*
    warfare; wars
armed force
and human security, 118–20, 132
and international security, 30, 31, 34, 61
armed humanitarian intervention, 137
Armitage, Richard, 101
arms control treaties, 32–3
'asymmetric warfare', 105–6
Augustine, Saint, 84
Auvinen, J., 103

Bajpai, Kanti, 119, 120
Baylis, John, 23
Beitz, Charles R., 41
Bellamy, Alex J., 126
Bible: and pacifism, 79
Bohman, L., 48, 55
Bonser, M., 126, 132
Boutros-Ghali, Boutros, 142, 144
Brock, P.,78, 79, 80, 83, 85, 86

Brown, Chris, 12, 45, 46, 128
Brown, Gary D., 67, 72
Buchanan, A., 41
Bull, Hedley, 14, 18, 30, 34, 37, 50, 102
Bush, George W. *see* United States

Cady, Duane L., 77, 81
Calhoun, Laurie, 67, 69
Canada: and peacebuilding, 115
Canadian Peacebuilding Coordinating
    Committee (CPCC), 145, 146
Carr, E. H., 42, 64
casualties: civilians *see* civilians'
    immunity to war
Catholic Relief Service, 146
Ceadel, Martin 77, 83
Charvet, John, 41
Chesterman, Simon, 130, 151
China: and state sovereignty, 128
Chomsky, Noam, 132
citizens: states' duties towards, 18, 35, 37
citizenship, 49
civil society: and cosmopolitanism, 49,
    87, 121–2
civil wars, 94, 97, 106
    Afghanistan, 27–8, 37, 106, 107, 118,
        150–1, 153
    Mozambique, 147–50
    Rwanda, 154
    Somalia, 94, 103–4, 134–5
    Spain, 80
    Sri Lanka, 97–101, 103
    Sudan, 96–7
civilians' immunity to war, 31–2, 52, 53,
    54–5, 63, 69–71, 82, 95–6, 115, 136

clans: Somalia, 104
Clausewitz, Karl Marie von, 14
Coates, A. J., 63, 65, 66, 67, 68, 72, 74, 76, 80, 83, 84, 85
coercion: and cosmopolitan law, 51
Cold War, 77–8
Commission on Human Security, 113, 114, 116, 117, 120
communitarianism, 15–16, 49, 74
and cosmopolitanism, 40, 41–2, 54
and human rights, 36
communities: embedded cosmopolitanism, 53, 54
conflict management see humanitarian intervention; ONUMOZ (United Nations Operation in Mozambique); peacebuilding; peace-keeping, UN; UN (United Nations): Protection of Civilians in Armed Conflict; United States: military intervention by
conflict resolution see humanitarian intervention; treaties
conscientious objection, 82; see also pacifism
consequentialism, 54, 56n
constitutionalism, 51
constructivism, 21
Cook, Robin, 129–30
cosmopolitan democracy, 50–1, 127
cosmopolitan law, 47–8
cosmopolitan values, 141
cosmopolitanism, 1, 3–4, 5, 6–7, 22–3, 33, 34, 87, 88, 93, 155, 159
characteristics of, 40–2
and communitarianism, 40, 41–2, 54
and discourse ethics, 44–5
and human rights, 36, 37, 55, 137
and human security, 120–3
and just war theory, 73, 157–8
and morality, 40–1, 43–4
and post-modern war, 106–8
see also embedded cosmopolitanism; impartialist cosmopolitanism
criminality, 104–5, 107
customs (state behaviour), 27

democracy, 80
Mozambique, 148, 149
Rwanda, 154
see also cosmopolitan democracy
'democratic peace theorem', 27
deontology, 56n
deontological ethics, 54
deontological normative theories, 42
development see human development
disappearances: Sri Lanka, 100
discourse ethics: and cosmopolitanism, 44–5
double effect principle, 69–70
double morality see Neibuhr, Reinhold
Dower, N., 41, 43, 44, 53, 62, 63
due care, principle of, 70
Dunne, Timothy, 11, 13, 26, 112, 114, 121–2

economic goals: armed conflicts, 96, 97
economic sanctions, 68
egalitarian antimilitarism see socialist antimilitarism
egalitarianism, 41
elections see democracy
11 September 2001, 23, 93
embedded cosmopolitanism, 52–4, 55
Enlightenment, The: and pacifism, 76–7
Erasmus, Desiderius, 80, 81
Erskine, Toni, 41–2, 44, 52–4
ethnic cleansing, 95; see also clans: Somalia; Rwanda
European Union, 51

Falk, Richard, 105
feminism: and communitarianism, 42
feudal wars, 102
Fixdal, M., 131
force see armed force
foreign intervention: civil wars, 97
Frelimo (Mozambique Liberation Front), 147, 148, 149, 150
Frost, Mervyn, 20, 22, 30–1, 35, 36

Galtung, Johan, 142, 144
Gandhi, Mohandâs Karamchand (Mahatma), 83, 85
gender and peacebuilding, 146–7

Geneva Conventions, 31, 32, 69
genocide *see* ethnic cleansing
global civil society *see* civil society: and cosmopolitanism
global ethics *see* world ethics
globalisation, 22, 37, 94, 105, 107, 152
governance, 50–1
governments: and human rights, 47
Grotius, Hugo, 29, 30
group loyalties, 17; *see also* loyalties
Gulf War (1991), 67

Habermas, Jürgen, 44, 47, 48
Hampson, Fen Osler, 111, 113, 114–15, 120, 121, 135
Hataley, T. S., 122
Held, David, 40, 41, 44, 47, 50, 51
Hoffman, S., 135
Holliday, Ian, 64, 66, 68
Howard, Michael, 103
Hubert, D., 126, 132
human development, 117–18
*Human Development Report* (UNDP), 112, 114, 118
human rights
    and cosmopolitan ethics, 45, 47, 49, 55, 121–2
    and human security, 114, 126, 136
    and self-defence, 131–2
human rights law, 35–6, 37; *see also* civilians' immunity to war
human rights treaties, 117–18
human rights violations, 65, 95
human security, 5, 44, 111–23
humanitarian intervention, 5–6, 55, 126–38, 158
humanitarian law, 37, 115; *see also* international law
humanitarian motives, 132–3
humanitarian pacifism, 81, 82

identity-based conflicts, 97, 104
impartialist cosmopolitanism, 52
impartiality, 41, 42
India: and Sri Lanka, 99–100; *see also* Gandhi, Mohandâs Karamchand 'Mahatma'

individualism, 49, 50
industrialisation of war *see* warfare, mechanisation of
interests of states, 21
International Bill of Rights, 117
international communities, 66–7
international law, 2, 26–9, 31, 34, 35, 47, 72, 78–9, 115, 117, 128, 129–31, 157
international politics, 11
    and morality, 15–19
    and war, 13
international relations: political realism, 15
internationalism, 1, 2, 4, 5, 22–3, 37, 49, 81–2
    and international law, 26–9, 35
    and pacifism, 79, 81
    and post-modern war, 107–8
    and security, 30
Iraq, 67, 119, 130, 151–2

*jus ad bellum*, 62, 63–8, 73–4, 81, 131
*jus cogens see* 'peremptory norms'
*jus in bello*, 69–71, 82, 131, 137
just cause, 62, 63, 64–5
just war criteria, 62–72
just war theory, 1–2, 5, 18, 30–1, 52, 55, 61, 69, 72–4, 131–4, 157, 158
    and pacifism, 77, 81, 82, 84

Kaldor, Mary, 49, 95, 102, 103, 104, 105, 143, 144
Kant, Immanuel, 3, 43–4, 45, 46–8, 49–50, 80, 158
Kaufman, Whitley, 70
Keen, David, 96–7
Keohane, R. O., 41
killing: in war, 18, 78, 86; *see also* civilians' immunity to war
King, G., 112
Kivimäki, T., 103
Kloos, Peter, 100, 101, 103
Knudsen, T. B., 126, 127, 129, 134, 135
Kosovo, 65, 135, 136
Küng, Hans, 51

Lacina, B., 142, 153
landmines, 122
languages *see* official languages; Sri
    Lanka
Last, David, 146
'last resort' criterion, 68
Latham, Andrew, 94, 102, 104
law, 3, 16, 18–19; *see also* cosmopolitan
    law; international humanitarian
    law; international law; natural law;
    rule of law; treaties
'legitimate authority', 66, 67
legitimate targets: noncombatants *see*
    civilians' immunity to war
Lerche, Charles, 144, 146
'level of threat': noncombatants *see*
    civilians' immunity to war
loyalties, 53; *see also* group loyalties
Lutz-Bachman, M., 48, 55

Machiavellian states, 12, 13
McRae, Rob, 104, 118, 121
McSweeney, Bill, 111–12
Mayer, Peter, 78, 80–1, 82
Middle East, 105–6
militarism *see* armed humanitarian
    intervention
military force: and human security *see*
    armed force: and human security
military security, 15, 22, 118
military technology *see* warfare,
    mechanisation of
Mitchell, George, 143
modern wars, 102, 143
moral agents, 53; *see also* embedded
    cosmopolitanism
morality
    and cosmopolitanism, 40–1, 43–4
    and international politics, 15–19
    and war, 63, 64, 70–1, 83–4, 131
    *see also* just war theory; pacifism
Morgenthau, Hans, 13, 15, 16, 17, 19,
    31–2
Mozambique, 147–50, 152
Mueller, John, 107
Murray, C. J. L., 112

Nardin, Terry, 136
nation states
    and morality, 16
    and war, 20–1
national interest: states, 18
nationalism, 16, 17
    Sri Lanka, 99
NATO
    and just cause, 63, 64, 65, 70
    and Serbia, 135, 136
natural law, 28–9
negative peace *see* peace, negative and
    positive
Niebuhr, Reinhold, 17, 49, 84
neorealists, 12, 14
'new wars' *see* 'post-modern' wars
9/11 *see* 11 September 2001
noncombatant immunity *see* civilians'
    immunity to war
nonintervention *see* humanitarian
    intervention
nonviolence *see* pacifism
Norman, Richard, 71, 78, 82
normative theories, 22, 43
norms, 4, 16–17
    ethical, 41–2
    and just war theory, 31
    'peremptory', 28
    and states, 20, 28, 36
Nossal, K. R., 122
nuclear war, 77–8
Nussbaum, Martha, 43, 44

official languages: Sri Lanka, 98–9
ONUMOZ (United Nations Operation in
    Mozambique), 147, 148, 149
Ottawa Convention on landmines, 33
Ottaway, M., 142, 153

pacifism, 2, 5, 55, 76–88, 134–8, 157–8
Paris, Roland, 152, 153
patriotism, 17
peace, negative and positive, 143, 144,
    149, 151, 153–4
peacebuilding, 6, 115, 141–55
peacekeeping, UN, 126
'peremptory norms', 28

PoKempner, Dinah, 32
political realism, 1, 2, 4, 11–12, 16, 18, 19
    and human security, 116
    in international politics 12–13, 33
    and law, 29
    limits of, 19–23
    and war, 13–15, 83, 106–7
politics see international politics
Porter, Elisabeth, 146–7
positive peace see peace, negative and
    positive
positivism, 29
post-colonial states, 128
'post-modern' wars, 102–6, 141, 144, 153
poverty, 117
power see morality: and international
    politics
'privatisation' of war, 94, 95, 101, 104–5
Project Ploughshares, 94
proportionality, 54, 62, 63, 67, 68, 134–5
Protection of Civilians in Armed Conflict
    (UN), 115

Ramcharan, Bertrand, 122
Ramsbotham, Oliver, 144, 146
Ramsey, Paul, 71
Rawls, John, 56n, 82
realism see political realism
reason: human beings, 42
reformist pacifism, 86
religions
    and pacifism, 79
    Sri Lanka, 99
Renamo (Mozambique National
    Resistance), 147, 148
revolutionary pacifism, 86, 87–8
right intention, 62, 65, 132
risk: due care, 70
Robinson, Mary, 117
Rodin, David, 64
Rogers, Paul, 106
Rousseau, Jean-Jacques, 80
rule of law, 27, 44, 46–8
Russell, Bertrand Arthur William, 3rd
    Earl, 77, 78, 79, 80, 87
Russia: and state sovereignty, 128; see
    also Soviet Union

Rwanda, 154

sanctions see economic sanctions
Schetter, C., 153
Scott, Shirley, 27–8, 35, 36
sectarian pacifism, 82
security see human security; military
    security; state security
self-defence, 28, 37, 64, 65, 131–2
September 11 2001 see 11 September
    2001
Serbia, 65, 70, 134
Smith, D., 131
Smith, M. L. R., 94
socialist antimilitarism, 79–80, 81, 85–6
soft power: and human security, 119–20,
    121
soldiers: as legitimate targets, 71–2
Somalia, 94, 103–4, 134–5; see also
    African Peace Facility
sovereignty see state sovereignty
Soviet Union, 147, 148; see also Russia;
    Mozambique
Spanish Civil War, 80
Sri Lanka, 97–101, 103
state-building, 106–7, 154, 155
state failure, 102–6
state security, 13, 14–15, 18, 22, 30, 35,
    47
state sovereignty, 3, 12, 18, 20, 33, 34,
    35–6, 46, 48, 50, 51, 126–7, 134
states, 19, 33, 50
    behaviour of, 27–8, 112–13
    constitutional dependence of, 28
    and human security, 111–13, 122
    and identity, 21
    Machiavellian, 12, 13
    post-colonial, 128
    and self-defence, 64, 65
    and war, 13, 14, 66, 73, 85, 94, 102
    see also Westphalian model of the
    state
Stoics, 43–4
'structural violence', 116–17
Sudan, 96–7; see also African Peace
    Facility
sustainable human development, 115–16

terrorism, 23; *see also* Al Qaeda; Sri Lanka; 'war on terror'

The Hague Conventions, 31, 32

*Theory of Justice, A* (Rawls), 56n

threats: human security, 112, 117, 118

Tolstoy, Leo Nikolayevich, Count, 3, 79, 85, 86

transnational civil society, 108

treaties, 32–4
  on human rights, 117–18
  and just war theory, 31

Treaty of Westphalia (1648), 28; *see also* Westphalian model of the state

UN (United Nations), 6, 35, 48, 49, 114, 126, 141, 143, 150–1, 155
  *Protection of Civilians Armed Conflict* (1999), 115
  *see also* ONUMOZ (United Nations Operation in Mozambique)

UN Charter, 31, 33, 35, 37, 48–9, 62, 64, 78–9, 129, 142

UNDP (United Nations Development Programme), 112, 114, 119, 120

UN Security Council
  *Agenda for Peace, An* (1992), 142, 144, 145, 153

and humanitarian intervention, 130–1, 133

United States
  and human rights, 121
  military intervention by, 32, 37, 101, 118, 130, 134, 151, 155
  and 'war on terror', 105, 106, 150, 152

Universal Declaration of Human Rights, 47, 49

UNOHAC (United Nations Office of the Humanitarian Assistance Coordinator), 148

utilitarianism, 43, 45, 78

vocational pacifism *see* sectarian pacifism

Walzer, Michael, 26–7, 36, 64, 66, 70, 73–4, 132

'war on terror', 105, 119–20, 152; *see also* terrorism

War Resisters' International, 78

warfare
  'asymmetric', 105–6
  mechanisation of, 19

wars
  feudal, 102
  as foreign policy, 150
  institutionalisation of, 72–3
  modern, 102
  and morality, 63, 64, 70–1, 78–9, 83–4, 131
  nuclear, 77–8
  and political realism, 13–15, 20–1
  post-modern, 102–6, 141, 153
  *see also* armed conflicts; international politics; just war theory; war on terror

weapons, 65, 115

Wendt, Alexander, 21–2

Westphalian model of the state, 6, 7n, 12, 22, 28, 50, 73, 87, 141, 142–3

Wheeler, Nicholas, 69, 70, 112, 114, 121–2, 128, 131–2, 133, 134, 137

Wight, Martin, 12, 13, 14, 15, 16, 20, 29–30, 48, 84, 85

Wimmer, A., 153

women *see* civilians' immunity to war; feminism: and communitarianism; gender: and peacebuilding

world ethics, 51

World Trade Center *see* 11 September 2001

World War I: pacifism, 80–1

Young, Nigel, 78, 79, 80, 83, 85, 86